Tea Light Moments to Refresh Your Day

Hope Lyda

HARVEST HOUSE PUBLISHERS

EUGENE, OREGON

Cover by Garborg Design Works, Savage, Minnesota

Cover photo © Garborg Design Works

TEA LIGHT MOMENTS TO REFRESH YOUR DAY
Copyright © 2009 by Hope Lyda
Published by Harvest House Publishers
Eugene, Oregon 97402
www.harvesthousepublishers.com

ISBN 978-0-7369-2408-5

Printed in the United States of America

09 10 11 12 13 14 15 16 / BP-SK / 10 9 8 7 6 5 4 3 2 1

Contents

Light a candle and wait upon God
to strengthen your faith.
Light a candle and pray for someone else
to shift your perspective.
Light a candle and lift up your hurts
to start your healing.
Light a candle and seek forgiveness
to transform your heart.
Light a candle and listen to God
to live your purpose.

❧

So now I can walk in your presence,
O God, in your life-giving light.

PSALM 56:13 NLT

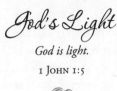

God's Light

God is light.

1 JOHN 1:5

Lighting a candle beckons me to sit still. The act is peaceful and inviting. So inviting that my impulse to work, finish tasks, make a call, or roam the house deciding what to do next is extinguished. I have an external focal point that leads to the internal...the soul, the heart. And here I discover, each time, the light of God.

In the past few years a spiritual and emotional journey led me back to the practice of lighting a candle to begin a time of focused prayer. To inspire the ritual, I placed a tea light candle in front of a framed image a friend had given to me for this journey. It is a beautiful woodcut based on a Gospel story in which Jesus raises a synagogue ruler's daughter from the dead. Above the scene are the Aramaic words *talitha cumi,* which mean "maiden, rise." Beneath the black-and-white contrasted image is the title "Come forth to life." I love that. Isn't that what we all long for? Whether we need joy, hope, mercy, or strength... the steps we take in faith are steps taken toward life. Abundant life. Intentional life. Meaningful life.

My prayers were initially for healing and direction; but over time, as I struck the match and leaned in toward the wick of the tea light candle in its glass holder, many other prayers and

---

thoughts would surface. This simple action reignited a desire to lift up my life completely to God's care.

I don't know what your journey looks like today, but I do know that the light of a single candle can help you find your way. It can lead you to times of prayer, meditation, questions, and praises. I invite you to light a candle and join me for a devotional pilgrimage through the mundane and the miraculous, the everyday and the eternal. May this gathering of observations, reflections, and prayers be a faithful companion for your life right now. I hope it inspires you to "come forth to life" in God and in meaningful ways.

Hope Lyda

From within or from behind, a light shines through us upon things, and makes us aware that we are nothing, but the light is all.

RALPH WALDO EMERSON

Light a Candle
for Connection

Potluck Faith

Who is greater, the one who is at the table or the
one who serves? Is it not the one who is at the
table? But I am among you as one who serves.

LUKE 22:27

I've had a strange, recurring idea lately. It involves clearing
away the living room furniture to make room for a cluster of tables. It requires the act of inviting people from different subgroups in my life to enter our home and share a meal
or two or three. This vision is especially crazy because I don't
cook. It's a bit uncomfortable because, as a personal rule of
thumb, I prefer solitary experiences over group ones. And it's
risky because I don't know who would show up and what the
event would be like.

What do you do with random "potluck" ideas that tug at
your heart? Are you someone who finds change difficult, even
when it seems to be God's leading? Numerous times I've resisted
the convictions of the heart. With my 20/20 hindsight, I see
how those were missed opportunities to grow and to inspire
others to grow.

Is God leading you toward connection with others in new
ways? How would following this call expand your life, enrich
it, complicate it, rescue it? When we say yes to opening up our
hearts, we often don't know what we'll get, but we do know

of a few certainties: We will discover new things about ourselves, others, and God's nature. We will be restless and even frustrated about changing the way we do things. And we will be scared. These are also the very reasons to join the mismatch gathering of hungry folks at God's table. You will fill up on strength, mercy, and wisdom…and you will be asked to share this feast with others.

Shedding Light

- How are you called to serve others or to create community? What keeps you from following this leading? Follow through with small ways to be more inclusive and to share your life.

- What are some of the most absurd ideas you wish you had followed through on in your past?

- What opportunity is rising up in your life right now that you want to embrace?

Prayer

God, lead my heart toward the uncomfortable ways of growth and the remarkable ways of hospitality. Rid me of my expectations and my desire to control the outcome so that I can overflow with your love. May I see every person as your child.

Afterglow

Today I will light a candle and enter God's presence. I will sit at his table, eager to be filled with his love and compassion for others.

Leaning into God

Truly, it is in the darkness that one finds the light,
so when we are in sorrow, then this
light is nearest of all to us.

MEISTER ECKHART

When we are feeling lonely, afraid, mildly anxious, or anything along the fear spectrum, we want connection with others. But we don't always know how to make that happen. I think the more isolated we are in our emotional state, the more we tend to wait for others to break through to us, to understand our emotional need or crisis, and to rescue us.

However, what we need to do is to reach out past our hurt or malaise and connect with others on our own initiative. It isn't easy to be vulnerable and open, is it? We learn to hold back those things that are unsettling or that might raise an eyebrow if expressed in certain "speak only of good things" company. Many of us have the same problem in our relationship with God. Instead of going to him with our needs, we wait for a thundering message to waken us from depression or an unbelievably great job offer to be extended to us by a stranger we meet in a Starbucks line. Those fantasies aren't nearly as powerful as our act of reaching out to God in our pain or need.

We'll learn how to receive help when we're willing to be vulnerable enough to share that need. There will be times when a discerning, prayerful friend shows up just when we need her. And there will be times when a conversation with a stranger does lead to something amazing. God acts on our behalf all the time. Leaning into his strength and leaning on his provision becomes our nature if we give ourselves to him openly and honestly each day (emotional mess days included). From those Mondays when we don't want to get out of bed to the days when a great loss leaves us unable to catch our breath...our first action only needs to be a conversation with God.

Shedding Light

- Is your pattern to wait for help instead of asking for it? Try to be more vulnerable in your communication with others, including God. Express your doubts and your needs, especially in prayer.

- Did you ever do a "trust fall" at camp or school? A person stands behind you and you fall back, trusting them to catch you. This is a great visual to have in mind when you pray. Imagine falling back as God catches you and your circumstance every time.

Prayer

I'm learning to be more open about my heartache and hopes. When I lean into your understanding and strength, I know you catch me each time. God, help me to trust more.

Afterglow

Today I will move toward vulnerability with someone I know. And tonight I will pray openly. I will confess my need for God.

Learning a New Language

If we use no ceremony toward others,
we shall be treated without any.

WILLIAM HAZLITT

To become fluent in a language, you not only learn vocabulary words and verb conjugations, you also study conversational customs and rhythm. When talking to a stranger or a business proprietor, Spanish speakers initiate conversation by making a personal connection. They ask how the other person is doing, and they wait for responses from the other person. These inquiries are not only pleasantries, but also extensions of respect, courtesy, and kindness. They are invitations to connect.

When I think of how task focused I have become in my interactions, it's a bit shameful. My mind usually skips past pleasantries and goes straight to an objective. I have many excuses: I feel scattered or forgetful much of the time, and I don't want to lose my train of thought (have you ever tried to stop a moving train?). Also, I'm a prime representative of a culture that is self-focused, in a hurry, and disconnected. My false sense of urgency overrides the need to connect with others at a personal, heart level. The problem is…I'm missing out on a lot of the dialogue of life.

To engage in true dialogue with another requires that we first offer up a bit of ourselves and then invite others to join the conversation. That can often be a scary, vulnerable, or time-consuming choice, but it is the most direct way to speak heart-to-heart with another. When we stop talking *at* others and start sharing *with* them, we achieve a deeper connection.

If you desire to become fluent in the language of faith, invite people to dialogue and stay long enough to learn a little something. Become an interpreter of the complex heart language. By all means, study your nouns and your verbs, but let us focus keenly on our adjectives: kind, caring, attentive, open, inviting, authentic.

Shedding Light

- Start a conversation with the intention of learning more about the other person or encouraging someone.

- The language of faith takes practice. Not so that it becomes rote, but so that it becomes authentic. Seek to be authentic in the words you choose and the way you respond to the comments of others. This will lead to deeper dialogue.

Prayer

God, let me speak to those I encounter with respect and consideration. Give me sensitivity to hear the needs of others, and give me patience to relate to and respond to what they aren't saying.

Afterglow

I'll make the effort to live out my verbs—love, listen, hear, accept, respond, believe, pray.

Add a Friend

Friendship marks a life even more deeply than love.
Elie Wiesel

For the longest time I resisted joining online communities. Then, when a good friend moved away, she encouraged me to make the leap into the ether playground. For someone who prefers to keep her personal life personal, I was surprised to see benefits to this public display of connection.

And then I was asked to "add a friend."

In "real" life I've become reluctant to add new relationships to my circle. Each friendship requires nurturing and attention (a good one, anyway), so I'm cautious. And now I'm supposed to add a friend of a friend? Or the guy who has something in common with someone I went to high school with? Well, okay... because this is what the world of multiplying cyberships is all about. It's a bit like asking everyone in your fifth grade class to be your valentine. It was a general gesture of friendship, no strings attached.

And then someone sent me a cyber fish.

And a tree and a kiss and a painting and a flower. And would I like to return the favor by sending a fish, a tree, a kiss, a painting, a flower? Now these were starting to feel like real relationships, the kind that take energy and effort. The ones I reluctantly add to my life. Sigh. But I've decided that this rabbit

---

trail party serves as a positive reminder that it can be enjoyable to "add a friend" without overthinking what's involved. Do you overthink friendships and pull back because of the responsibility?

Wouldn't God want us to "accept" rather than "decline" those people who do come into our lives daily? This is a lesson I'm still working on. Will you be my friend? I can promise you one thing…I'll never send you a fish.

Shedding Light

- Do you feel too limited by time and energy to pursue any more relationships? Try to welcome a new friendship into your life without evaluating it.

- Consider what you consider to be your community. How can you develop your connection to that community?

Prayer

Give me a desire to welcome new people into my life. I want to be able to accept others and share my life with them. When I want to build up my walls, my filters…remind me to remain open and generous with my time and my compassion.

Afterglow

I'll reach out to others more frequently. I'll engage in conversations and expand my community.

The Agenda of Authenticity

There is never any great achievement by the things of religion without a heart deeply affected by those things.

JONATHAN EDWARDS

Talking about beliefs that define us stirs up the emotions tied to those matters of significance. As it should be…we are passionate about anything that fuels our personal passions. But those emotions, so strong as they rise up, can overwhelm our message. If you have anything you want to present to others as true, as life-changing, or of importance to you…your primary agenda should be authenticity.

When we try to force a viewpoint, control conversations, or concoct situations so that we have a person "right where we want them," we sacrifice the chance to be a representative of our message and have settled for being a lobbyist. But a lobbyist, true to their moniker, always remains on the outside as they try to influence happenings on the inside.

Unfortunately, a lobbyist is left to rely on pressure and enticements as their bag of tricks. An emotional lobbyist is not able to enter the interior of a person's heart or circle of trust. Instead, become a representative for your important message. Share your heart; don't sell it. As you develop a relationship with another and witness what their needs are, then the door to their heart is open to receive you and to hear what matters to you. A lobbyist might gain power, but a representative gains understanding and credibility and the right to speak from their heart about those things that compel them. The bag full of tricks can be replaced with a heart that is full of truth, empathy, and compassion.

Shedding Light

- Are you trying to be a lobbyist for something you believe in? Stop forcing issues and start fueling relationships.
- The fastest way to become a representative is to become a listener. Practice listening in every situation. Stop offering up your solution at every lull in the conversation. Rest in the experience of getting to know someone. You will discover the best way to love that person.

Prayer

Lord, guide me to see what others bring to the table. When I think that I am always the teacher or the leader, I am sacrificing my chance to be a student. I want to see each new situation and each person I meet as an opportunity to learn more of your nature and your ways. Help me to rest in being a listener and a person who nurtures another's heart. This is how faith interacts with another. This is how compassion works.

Afterglow

I will toss aside my agenda so that I can catch a sense of compassion for others.

Strong Connection

Only when one is connected to one's inner core is
one connected to others. And, for me, the core, the
inner spring, can best be re-found through solitude.

ANNE MORROW LINDBERGH

Give me my space!" Have you ever wanted to shout this to
someone or pray it fervently to God after a long day? This
might seem like the cry of a distant, indifferent person, but there
is much value in the sacred act of creating space and resting in
solitude. Not so that we can distance ourselves from community and covenant with others, but so that we can take time to
restore our sense of peace and wellness as God's child.

When I take advantage of solitude to seek God's heart, I am
renewing my sense of connection with every person on earth.
When I light a candle and lift up the prayer that has gone unspo-
ken for days because I've been too distracted or self-centered,
I experience renewal, hope, and sensitivity toward others. We
come to God with our weary hearts and our specific praises and
petitions, and Abba graciously receives them and embraces us
with assurances and peace. And then something wonderful happens within the very core of our spiritual self...we see beyond
ourselves. We can walk among the masses and feel lonely, but
as we enter God's presence, we are no longer isolated in our
thoughts. We are given the security of his very real attention

and love, and we are guided to notice that we are a part of something so much bigger than our current concern.

As much as I lean toward being a loner, I know this can never be my identity. Because as soon as I slip into God's presence and think on how interconnected my life is with that of the stranger I passed at the coffee shop or the best friend I've had since high school…I get chills. This is the body of Christ. I'm a part of it. You're a part of it.

Shedding Light

- Allow yourself time in solitude along with silence. After you read a devotion, allow another ten minutes to pass in which you assign no specific task other than to meet God.

- Does the idea of solitude make your palms sweat and your mind soar with ways to sabotage any blip of alone time? Each round does not have to be in silence. Choose good background music for your time alone. Bake something. Whistle. Journal. Just let your thoughts be of and for God.

Prayer

Calm the pace of my heartbeat. Steady my thoughts. Ready my spirit. I want to experience your presence, God.

Afterglow

I'll figure out how to dedicate some of my alone time to seeing and seeking God.

Light a Candle
for Clarity

I Can See Clearly Now

*Saul headed toward Damascus. As he
came near the city, a bright light from
heaven suddenly flashed around him.*

ACTS 9:3 NCV

A glimpse of light can trigger within us a sense of hope and peace. It can illuminate the very best in our hearts. The symbolic flame of a wedding unity candle indicating two lives joined as one. The bright eyes of a child discovering the world around them. An advent candle lit to mark the holy season. The silvery white of an ultrasound image outlining the miracle of new life.

The most powerful, the most moving, the most transforming light is that of God's love. That can sound like a phrase pulled from an overused religious dictionary, but when we encounter the brilliant purity of mercy, the cliché ends and the Christ experience begins.

I have a fondness for the exciting story of Saul's conversion on the road to Damascus. I don't find it overly dramatic or hard to embrace as truth. To me, it makes perfect sense that Saul, a persecutor of Christians and vehement hater of Christ, encountered his road to conversion, his path to faith, and his way to clarity with the help of a blinding light.

When God casts his light on our lives, the shadows are

exposed. We notice the dirt of sin, the smudges of bad judgment, and the wounds of our brokenness, and we realize how off course our lives have been. Then, in a flash of grace, those blemishes and regrets are washed away. Our new vision reveals the way to the hope, peace, and faith of a transformed life. We just have to walk forward.

Shedding Light

- What is God shedding light on in your life right now? How will this transform your faith from this day forward?

- Step out of the shadows that have darkened your life in the past. What will this freedom mean to you?

Prayer

God, your light guides me to ways and thoughts of peace. You've transformed me with grace, and you've illuminated my path of purpose. Help me live in the light so that my shadows are revealed, and I am able to live a transformed life. Amen.

Afterglow

I will walk forward in grace and will celebrate my encounter with God's love.

An Awakened Faith

*They have eyes to see but do not see and
ears to hear but do not hear.*

EZEKIEL 12:2

When I get run down or overly stressed, a haze covers my thoughts and I react in slow motion. I lack control of my body. My arms and legs don't feel like my own. A friend will point to a big bruise and ask what happened, and I shrug my foggy "I dunno" shrug. More times than not, the bruise was formed when I walked into the rocking chair or hit my hand against the buffet in the dining room, both of which have been in the same locations for years.

Unfortunately, these times of weariness and emotional survival can cause more than a bruised knee. These times of internal processing and disconnect from my outer world cause me to be careless with my words, comments, and attitude. I stop watching for and listening for God's direction. I don't have the energy to care about what unfolds each day or who about me has needs. The social and spiritual filters I should use to determine when something I'm about to say is helpful or hurtful are defective. My careless responses and remarks can bruise the feelings of those in my path. I don't listen very patiently to my husband. I become more blunt than honest with friends. And my social graces all but disappear when I have to mix and mingle or just make it through the 15-items-or-less line.

When we are spiritually worn out or hard-hearted, we will also experience this time of wandering aimlessly, in a haze. We become careless with our hearts and our sense of truth, and we tend to run into obstacles more frequently. It is as important to find ways to stay spiritually alert as it is mentally alert. The way to health in both categories can be similar. Pray more/rest more. Get fed spiritually/eat healthily. Make time for fellowship/take time for friendships. Break away for spiritual reflection/give yourself a break. This will lead to your awakening.

Care more about this life you're walking through…it is physical *and* spiritual…and nothing less.

Shedding Light

- How has your spiritual and physical life shown signs of weariness?

- What has caused the most heart bruises in your life?

- How can you use this time of refreshment to restore clarity and hope? Why do you want to be "awake" in your faith and life?

Prayer

Remove this haze from my life, God. I want to be fully aware of each day and each opportunity to grow in my understanding of faith and hope. You provide rest for this weary child of yours. Thank you.

Afterglow

I will start each day with a focused prayer, asking for eyes to see and ears to hear. I don't want to miss the life God is showing me.

The Real Thing

Hold a true friend with both your hands.

NIGERIAN PROVERB

Like any relationship, a friendship can run on empty when one or both parties have to work too hard to keep it running. As we mature and discover more about ourselves, it can be important to evaluate the health of our friendships. Do some friends feed your soul, while others continually undermine your heart and purpose? Do some withhold their kindness and appreciation, while others express a continuous outpouring of support? Are you striving to see the best in others, or do you project your own struggles and weaknesses on to them?

We sometimes seek out friends who fill a certain void. They might be the listener we never had as a child or the leader who takes charge of our follower personality. Friendships can grow between a mentor and a mentee or between coworkers or people who are placed in the same location at the same time during a pivotal point in their lives. But these connections aren't always enough to sustain a long-term, healthy friendship. These connections, however, do allow for us to learn from each person who crosses our paths. Each interaction, friendship, and association is our opportunity to recognize goodness in another. Lasting friendships require an investment of ourselves.

As you give all of your relationships a checkup this year, don't forget to examine your friendship-ability. The things you need from others are very likely the things they need from you. This clarity will help you value the people in your life and be grateful for those who have been a part of it along the way.

Shedding Light

- Are you the friend you want others to be?
- How have you aligned yourself with people who are healthy for you/not healthy for you?
- See each relationship in your life with new eyes. Focus on the goodness that each person offers.

Prayer

I want a pure heart, God. Help me to hold back feelings of judgment or envy. Give me a desire to see the good in everyone. If there are people in my life who are hurtful, give me the strength to truly see those situations so that there can be healing.

Afterglow

I will welcome each person in my life with an embrace of acceptance and grace. And I will let go of those who are destructive so that there can be healing.

Beneath the Surface Tension

Ciúnas gan uaigneas

(Gaelic for "quietness without loneliness")

Busyness keeps us operating in stress mode. When we awaken to an overflowing mental in-box, our thoughts shift to immediate tasks, daily goals, and hourly survival needs. We remain on the surface level of our spiritual and emotional lives. An inquiry from a friend about how we are doing might lead us to dig a bit deeper for a few moments, but quickly our personal filters shift us back to surface dialogue. While writing a reflective email, we might contemplate our more significant needs, but a new email arrives and we return to the tricky business of juggling tangents.

Lighting a candle and spending moments in silence gives you time to explore who you are apart from today's emergent needs. You can't ignore what is on your plate because that is what you do when you're living in the present. But if your present never involves excavating thoughts that go beyond immediate needs, in-the-moment grumbles, and brief-encounter small talk, you will eventually disconnect from your heart, spirit, and God's leading from within. What might appear to be a well-managed life to the world is more often a life held together purely by surface tension. One break in the constant noise, the anxious routine, and everything will spill. Learn to be still and quiet without feeling alone. God is in that stillness.

Sit in silence for a time of prayer and exploration as you sink into the ideas, feelings, and dreams you've been ignoring. Make time to breathe and to question the way things are going and to take note of what you feel. Break through that surface tension and enjoy riding the waves of possibility that will flood over you. You will be refreshed and reminded how exciting it is to live a deeper life connected to God and his leading.

Shedding Light

- Give yourself the gift of knowing your heart more intimately.
- Do you feel alone when you take a moment to be quiet? Discover the companionship and comfort of the quiet by introducing the practice of solitude and prayer into your life.

Prayer

Why do I run from silence? The peace of a still moment? I know you are there, Lord, waiting for me to express my life and to listen to your leading and whispers of grace.

Afterglow

I will introduce five minutes of quiet time into my life each day this week, and I will increase that time by one minute each following week.

Growing a Problem

Some people are making such thorough plans
for rainy days that they aren't enjoying today's sunshine.

WILLIAM FEATHER

With a handful of snow and a fresh trail of more white ahead, I can easily turn a wimpy cluster of water and air into a rather large, dense mass. I spent a childhood indulging in this metamorphic process of turning a small lump into a large mound. Given the right conditions, I could even grow that small lump into the impressive bulges of a life-sized snowperson. Maybe this is why I am so diligent at rolling small problems around in fresh patches of thought. Each roll adds weight and mass, giving the problem a much more substantial position in my mind. When my conditions are just right for negativity—a bad experience, an anxious heart, naysayers around me, or a rough self-image day—that hypothetical what-if? is no longer miniscule but looks life sized and rather daunting. It is so big, in fact, that it can cast a shadow on today's decisions, attitude, and perspective.

Is there a mass of what-ifs you are rolling around in your mind with vigor and determination? Isn't it amazing how it can actually *feel* productive to grow our problems? I've realized over the years that if I let some sunshine in, these growing blobs begin to disappear. Positive thoughts, prayer, prayers of others, encouraging readings, enjoyable activities, and friendships will warm up my thoughts and start to shift the internal storm toward a brighter day. The next time you roll the same old problems around a new day's worth of clean thoughts, step into the warmth of good thinking and positive actions. It is so much better to see your problems melt down and avoid a mental meltdown of your own.

Shedding Light

- How have you snowballed a possible problem into a certain obstacle?

- Why do you think you bring old problems or worries back into each day's new thoughts? Where did you learn to do this? Do you worry what would fill your mind if you let go of these old patterns?

Prayer

I'm so tired of these anxieties and hypothetical problems, God. I know I waste the provision of each day on these useless worries. Help me to let go of them and to see them for what they are… obstacles I myself have created. I want to see how my life will be filled with goodness when I let go of fear.

Afterglow

When old worries pop into my mind today, I will say "today is for the light of new thoughts" and will feel the old melt away.

Imperfect Offerings

Give all thou canst; high Heaven rejects the lore
Of nicely-calculated less or more.

WILLIAM WORDSWORTH

It is an unexpected gift. I stare at the sweet little bird with a sunshine yellow belly and soft, gray feather tufts on its head. This early morning gift has been given with the utmost affection, and yet it saddens me. You see, this tiny bird has been left on my doorstep by my very proud and adoring cat, Katie. I shake my head. I so hate to see the bird population drop by one victim a week, but I also understand that this happens when cats encounter winged beings. I happen to know that Katie isn't starving because I frequently fill her ceramic dish with triangle-shaped dry food. The purpose of her hunting excursion is to express her nature and, I believe, to present us with her portion of the mortgage. As sad as it makes me, this is her offering.

As I dispose of the bird, I have a moment of clarity about my offerings to God. Many times I've substituted something that would truly please God—my commitment, faithfulness, time, undivided attention—for the remains of something I pursued out of my nature—halfhearted joy, a reluctant tithe, a wimpy effort to extend compassion, etc. I don't even have the disclaimer of sincere kitty-pride as I lay my weak gifts out before God with a groan of embarrassment.

How many times have your choices saddened God? Last week, did he pick up your failed attempt to forgive with a rubber-gloved hand, shake his head, and add it to the pile of past offerings with a sigh? Pay attention to what you are pursuing with all of your heart and soul. It might be more about what interests you than about what pleases God.

Shedding Light

- Take a look at those gifts you place on God's porch week after week. Are they about you or about God?
- When do you give of yourself completely? Is it in one area of your life or during certain times of your life? Ask yourself why you hold back in other arenas or during other times.

Prayer

God, I'm sorry for the times when I lift up my stuff, my desires, my pursuits and call them offerings. I know I often give you the remains of my failed efforts rather than the whole of me. May I learn to put aside my nature so that I can adopt your nature and your heart for life and others.

Afterglow

Today I'll watch for opportunities to give out of a desire to please God rather than myself.

Light a Candle
for Gratitude

Highlights

Light tomorrow with today.

ELIZABETH BARRETT BROWNING

I had a good math teacher who had one flaw—he always used sports scenarios to explain mathematical principles. Yet here I am about to jump into a sports analogy. First, I'll preface it with this: I'd rather sit on nails than sit through a full game of televised football. However, I can tolerate watching the highlights on the weekend sports shows. Watching a 15-minute compilation of a week's worth of sports makes sense to me. Show me the good stuff. Show me who made great moves and saved the day. Point out a team's progress and then show me the scores and rankings. It's very uplifting to see clip after clip of good plays. The spiritual lesson? If we were given the opportunity to watch, every weekend, our personal highlights of the week, would we be inspired? Would there be enough material to even fill the sports show format?

When I think of highlights, I think in terms of successful passes and catches. Giving and receiving. Simple enough. Did you give words of praise to others? When a friend tried to tell you about their struggle, did you receive their words with tenderness and care? Highlights also reveal how a play was supposed to go and then how it was carried out, for better or for worse. If we diagrammed our actions for a week, would the white chalk marks look like a kindergartner's sugar-induced drawing or would they show that we were following the plan given to us by a higher authority?

I think we would all benefit from the opportunity to review our lives now and then. Play by play. Decision by decision. Move by move. We'll have fewer fumbles when we understand that we are given our position and our ability for a higher purpose…so that we can heed God's calls daily and create a life filled with highlights tomorrow. Go team.

Shedding Light

- How do you spark the light of hope for others?
- When were you last inspired by the words or actions of another? Consider how you can model them. Ask God what you have to give today and give it.

Prayer

So many fumbles, Lord! I have many regrets, but now I want to see each day as my chance to serve you, bring about light for others, and inspire the hearts of friends and strangers with simple kindnesses.

Afterglow

To follow God's plan for my day, I will watch closely for ways to make the most of the day and to build up others.

Daily Sacraments

For everything that lives is holy, life delights in life.

WILLIAM BLAKE

I went to a local restaurant and ordered a very basic meal of rice, black beans, veggies, and chicken with a dash of salsa. I gave my name with my order to the manager at the counter, and I retreated to a corner table to wait. A few minutes later, I saw the man step out from the kitchen. He called out my name and I stood up to meet him halfway. I reached for my take-out container, and as I did, the manager paused and communicated what my order was. As he carefully listed off the ingredients, they each sounded rich and satisfying. I nodded my thanks, received the cardboard container, and headed out the door to walk several blocks back home. All the while I was thinking about how his presentation of the meal felt like an offering of the sacraments. His manner and our exchange made my ordinary order feel important and personal.

My take-out meal was healthy but it wasn't remotely holy. This sacrament wasn't communion. And yet, this moment of simple generosity and attention revealed how we can transform ordinary exchanges into meaningful acts of grace. When our manner is deliberate and gentle, we meld the sacred with the everyday. We can do this for others in our lives. Saying grace before dinner will make the time shared over that meal more special. Shaking hands with a stranger as we ask their name will make our connection more personal. Asking how someone is and caring about the answer will expand our relationships.

Take time to slow down and have genuine exchanges with people. Whether you are giving or receiving, do so with a grateful heart. And when you can, be sure to list off the ingredients that blend to create your good life…make this an offering of thanks to God.

Shedding Light

- How can you bring the sacred into your daily life?
- When have you witnessed a moment that melded the sacred with the ordinary? How did it make you feel?
- What are your main obstacles to nurturing holiness and goodness? Busyness, self-importance, surface living, uncertain how to begin?

Prayer

Show me how to express my awe in your goodness and grace, God. Lead me to seek out ways to honor faith and to serve you. Give me your heart for others so that generosity and hospitality become my way of interaction.

Afterglow

I will enter my day with the word "sacred" on my mind. I will give and receive the daily sacraments of grace and belief.

Benediction of Gratitude

*We need to remind each other that the cup of sorrow
is also the cup of joy, that precisely what causes us
sadness can become the fertile ground for gladness.*

HENRI NOUWEN

"Today is the day the Lord has made; let us rejoice and be glad in it." My husband calls this out in the morning. If I haven't hit my snooze alarm thrice, I call out "Amen" in response. And I mean it. Awe and pride both rise up when I hear this morning blessing because I know Marc is choosing to sip from the cup of gratitude. And he is sharing that cup with me. Who am I to refuse to drink? I have not faced the hardships he has in the past few years. I have supported him, I have stood by him, I have prayed for him, but I have not faced the physical trial that has been his journey. The gifts of compassion, prayer, and generosity I have known during this trial lead me to the cup. When I witness my husband's willingness to celebrate a day, not because it is easy but because it is a gift from God, then I am compelled to lift the cup to my lips.

If we reject gratitude until we experience a perfect day or our life becomes an uncomplicated bliss-fest, then we will not partake of it. Perhaps ever. You don't produce gratitude. Success doesn't produce gratitude. Gratitude comes from God. Do you recognize that your present reason for perseverance is also a reason to be grateful? Can you face a future of unknowns, standing on some hard-to-face knowns, and still rejoice in the possibility of hope and goodness? Will you give your heartache to God so that something meaningful can be made from your pain? If so, then you have come to the cup of gratitude. Drink. Today *is* the day the Lord has made; let us rejoice and be glad in it. Can I hear an "amen"?

Shedding Light

- What have you let keep you from sipping from the cup of gratitude?

- Find ways to open up your life to receive it. Consider focused times of prayer or journaling. Create lists of what you are thankful for this week, this season.

Prayer

I've wanted my trials to be taken from me, and yet they lead me to the cup of gratitude. I am ready to be filled and renewed.

Afterglow

I will see gratitude not as a reflection of my circumstances, but as a response to my God.

Change of Tune

Change your thoughts, and change your world.

NORMAN VINCENT PEALE

Did you get one too? That broken record...the one that sticks on negative phrases and repeats them over and over? How did so many of us end up buying into a faulty record? Maybe it ended up as a white elephant gift and we've all attended too many holiday or company parties. The great news is that mental records, just like the physical ones, can be replaced by remixed downloads.

Light a candle for this round. Now let the record play. Listen to the lists of perceived faults or mistakes. Don't forget the one about how you don't make good choices, never have, never will. And let's see what else...you can't lose weight because you're lazy. Or, you can't try something new because you're not smart enough. Dig into your broken record collection from way back. The oldies but goodies. Maybe comments from your parents or from a friend who made herself feel better by putting you down? If your home was governed by anger, do you re-create that world with your self-talk and your actions? If your family struggled financially or emotionally, do you tell yourself you're destined for the same?

This is your chance to toss out the broken pieces and download thoughts of love, blessing, and healing. Today, for every

---

negative chorus you can list, think of something you are grateful for, something you are good at, something you have set as a goal, and something you know to be true about God's love for you—which is so great and deep that it replaces the shame and the sin, the harm and the hurt, the tears and the transgressions.

You are not going through your old broken records in order to dust them off and keep them handy in your life today. This is your chance to say goodbye. And as your connection to God becomes stronger, the list of reasons to be grateful will rise to the surface of your mind and spirit. God's promises will play, over and over, and your heart will be glad.

Shedding Light

- I know you can quote the bad stuff. It's inscribed on your heart. Let yourself throw away those records.

- Have you passed along your broken sayings and beliefs to others? Restore in them a sense of joy and gratitude by building them up and modeling for them God's grace.

Prayer

Forgive me for replacing your love and truths with the lies I tell myself. I think I even speak negative words in my sleep. God, I am grateful for your words of healing and mercy. They fill me with hope. Amen.

Afterglow

I will enjoy a morning, a day, a week of thinking differently and believing in God's love.

Drawing from the Well

Once we have only God to depend on...
then we can with joy "draw water out of
the wells of salvation" (Isaiah 12:2-3).

CATHERINE MARSHALL

Imaginary Counselor: You seem to have a lot on your mind.

You: I have to juggle a lot these days. I can't keep track, and it overwhelms me. Life is hard and complicated and...

IC: And?

You: Lonely.

IC: How is your giving these days?

You: I told you. I have a lot to juggle.

IC: Maybe you're holding on to too much.

You: What's the alternative?

IC: Give to others. Share your burdens and your blessings.

You: What would I have to offer right now?

IC: Time. Kindness. Service. A welcome smile. An offer of support. A phone call.

You: Those things you listed...I need them!

IC: Start giving from a place of gratitude.

You: I told you…life is hard. I don't know that I'm really…

IC: Grateful?

You: Yes. That sounds so awful. I used to thank God for my blessings. I don't know what happened.

IC: You tried to generate gratitude from your own reserves, from your own circumstances, and you couldn't. Gratitude comes from the well of God's heart. It never runs dry. In fact, it overflows. Are you going to be renewed in your gratitude?

You: I'm ready to draw from the well of God's love and grace. What do I do?

IC: Start giving.

Shedding Light

- Are you willing to give even when you are in a place of hardship?

- I've had to rely on God's well of grace and gratitude. I know he is faithful. Bring your pail and join me here.

Prayer

Lord, I will come to your heart, your love, and, abundance to draw what I need…not only so that I can be filled, but so that I can share with others.

Afterglow

I will act out my belief that God's love is endless and that his grace flows without limit.

Light a Candle
for Peace

Faith in Faith

He said to me, "My grace is sufficient for you,
for my power is made perfect in weakness."

2 CORINTHIANS 12:9

I t can happen like this: On a Monday we are doing well and feeling secure about life and our place in the world. We pray, we believe, we lean on God. On a Wednesday we encounter a sorrow that shakes our foundation of faith. By Saturday we are trying to process our difficult circumstance and regain our balance and keep on moving in our original direction, but it isn't easy to move forward when you are reaching out to stabilize yourself with every step you take. It is deeply painful to question God's care or God's presence, but I believe these times of conflict happen to many of us. Having faith might just be the most difficult, perpetual action we could commit to.

What we need to say to those who are experiencing times of doubt and spiritual chaos—and what we personally need to hear when we are struggling—is that it is sufficient to have faith in faith for this time. When your mind is scattered and you spend sleepless nights picking apart everything you believe, from your sense of self to your sense of the Creator, it is okay to turn to and rest in the heart knowledge of faith's power. While we might not believe it during times of sadness or hardship, it is through such storms that we become more certain that

God's love is real. God doesn't stand on the other side of the chasm of belief and watch you struggle. God is willing to be in the struggle with you, even if you don't understand how grace works, even when you become cynical about the possibility of unconditional love, and especially when you wonder if you have what it takes to trust completely.

You don't have to have all the answers to the questions right now...but you do need one answer. Yes, faith in faith alone is enough for right now.

Shedding Light

- How can having faith in faith free you from your burden of uncertainty during hard times?
- Do you put too much pressure on yourself to have all of the answers...the God-answers of life? You might be trying to replace faith with knowledge and control. Return to faith.

Prayer

Resting in faith sounds so good to me. My heart has been broken, and I don't understand life right now. Why do I try to figure out everything and fix everything in my own power? I am tired and uncertain. I have moments of doubt. Give me rest today, God. For today, it is enough to have faith in faith.

Afterglow

Through prayer, I will exchange my control, doubt, and pain for the peace of faith.

Nothing Too Great

*All we are asked to bear we can bear. That is a
law of the spiritual life. The only hindrance to the
working of this law, as of all benign laws, is fear.*

ELIZABETH GOUDGE

After some years of expending significant energy, time, and effort toward one area of life, I feel weary. Have you been through a season of depletion? Did you lose hope or love? Physically, such a time is demanding. You crave heavy sleep that carries you through dream after dream, yet rest comes only in fits and starts. Spiritually, such a time is distancing. You want connection to God, yet intimacy is elusive.

These times of emptiness become experiences of healing and peace. God longs for us to be whole and complete. Our circumstances may have taken away something of great importance in our lives, but when we offer our hearts to God as empty, hurting vessels, he fills them until they can hold no more. Healing can be painful. As peace pours back into our lives, it will stretch our hearts and dreams. We have to relearn what it feels like to be replete with God's love and satiated with the sweetness of hope.

When you spend sleepless nights and difficult days measuring your emptiness, do not worry that its dimensions are too great for your human efforts to ever fill. No pain or weariness

is too big to be brought to the Source of your joy and healing.
God's mercy will keep on flowing until pain is replaced by peace
and your loneliness is replaced by lasting communion.

Shedding Light

- Do you believe that God is greater than the hurt you feel?
- When has fear pulled you back into the emptiness?
- What do you hope for in God? Healing, rest, peace,
  answers, forgiveness? He offers these to you.

Prayer

Fill me with your love, God. Replace the ache of pain with the
ease of peace. I've held back my hurt because I saw no way
around it or through it. You are that way. Lead me into your
mercy.

Afterglow

I will let go of the physical or spiritual trial that has emptied my
heart and ask to be filled with hope.

Borrowed Longings

*The really important things are not houses
and lands, stocks and bonds, automobiles and
real estate, but friendships, trust, confidence,
empathy, mercy, love and faith.*

BERTRAND RUSSELL

Our moods, priorities, and decisions can be swayed by a very important factor. I'm not talking about our diet or finances. I'm looking at a more internal force: our longings. What are you striving to accomplish or become? Do you crave attention and love? Have you always wanted a large family? Do you long for a big house with a perfect yard? Are there days you wish you were in a different marriage or a new family entirely?

Longings can draw us closer to our purpose if they are directed toward God. When our hearts long for God's love and for his grace to sweep over our lives, we are looking for healing and a chance to belong. But when our longings become a persistent grumble, one long sigh of dissatisfaction, then they are no longer tied to our dreams and our purpose but are anchored to malcontent and the world's sense of fulfillment and entitlement. In fact, I think more than a few of us are carrying a sense of regret or envy over things that aren't even our longings to begin with. We listen to the expressed dissatisfaction of our peers, coworkers, celebrities, or friends, and soon our life that seemed fine the day before is, over time, cast in a gloomy shade of gray. This is when we truly believe that life would be better, if not perfect, in that house, with that spouse, with those clothes, in that car, near that beach, in that size dress.

Notice where daydreams take your heart and be willing to go deeper. When you're frustrated about a situation or a relationship, consider whether you are measuring it up against someone else's version of the good life. Redirect your longings toward the things of God—compassion, love, patience, perseverance, kindness, and integrity. These desires will not mislead you. They will fill your life and satisfy your heart.

Shedding Light

- Whose longings are you striving to fulfill? Have you borrowed a few from parents, friends, our culture?
- Which godly longings would you like to focus on?
- Which borrowed longings are you ready to let go of?

Prayer

I realize I live my life with a twinge of discontentment because I'm pursuing things that have nothing to do with my purpose. God, give me a peace for those pursuits that are of you and your direction for me.

Afterglow

I will pursue the dreams that have my name on them…the dreams that are shaped for me by a personal God.

Open Windows

The windows of my soul I throw
Wide open to the sun.

JOHN GREENLEAF WHITTIER

One rainy Thursday night, I was walking along an urban residential block enjoying the darkening sky of dusk. An ambulance siren shrieked at a nearby hospital. A car alarm sounded two blocks over. And an electric streetcar heading north whirred on its tracked course behind me. These sounds all faded from my attention as I approached an old brick apartment building and heard an appealing song being played somewhere overhead. I glanced into the drizzle and saw an open window a couple of floors up. A single light was on. I could hear two girls laughing and talking above the music coming from speakers somewhere just inside the ornately trimmed sill. If I could go by their music choice, I'd bet that these girls have great taste in food, friends, and movies.

I like what open windows can offer a passerby. When we open up our souls to those who pass by and through our lives, there is a lot we can share in a matter of moments. If we project an authentic bit of who we are to each person we encounter, we will offer them a glimpse of who God is and what God is doing through us. Let's hope they sense warmth, kindness, and peace. Let's pray they hear the good music of praises and wisdom. And when sadness is raining on their lives, may the other sounds fade to the background as they hear the gentle music of our hearts welcoming them to friendship, laughter, and a warm place to be themselves.

Shedding Light

- Do you open up the windows to your soul so that others see who you are?

- Are you one to quickly invite another to an authentic conversation, sincere laughter, and genuine connection? Or do you keep a barrier between you and others until they have proven themselves in some way?

Prayer

You bring joy and peace into my life, God. In those moments when I make a connection with another person, I feel a sense of connection to you. Show me when and how I hold back my true self so that I can open up and be willing to extend a generous heart and a listening spirit to another.

Afterglow

I will watch for and welcome opportunities, people, connection, possibility, leading, and the peace of an open life and faith.

Missing Peace

God can make you everything you want to be,
but you have to put everything in His hands.

MAHALIA JACKSON

What is missing from your life? There are two extreme ways that some people think on this question: They build a life around their personal answer. Whether their void is loneliness or value or love, they focus on that one area with such determination that they sacrifice other areas. Or they build a life focused on the question itself. They don't know what is missing, but they do know they don't have peace. Their quest to answer the question becomes a singular journey that doesn't lead very far and the answer is always out of reach.

This question usually sneaks up on us when we face a transition or when we observe someone else's change in season: a new baby, a graduation, a funeral. You might try to shake it the way you would a tagalong younger sibling, but when you acknowledge what is missing you can begin to pray for that area daily.

I'm talking a lot about the question and less about the answer because we each have a different void, a different bit of longing which will vary as our life circumstances change. But if we trace the missing piece back to its root—the desire for love, the need for security, the hope of healing—we can rest in the answers we are given by our Creator. Unconditional love, the assurance of grace, the promise of wholeness.

The peace-filled life is not one large puzzle that requires precisely shaped or colored pieces; the peace-filled life is fluid, beautiful, and abundant. Have you been so focused on getting married or accomplishing a career goal or having a kitchen with green marble tiles that you haven't asked and answered the important question: "Am I ready to let go of the missing piece in order to have God's peace?"

Shedding Light

- Have you pursued one aspect of life with such fervency that you've sacrificed other areas?

- When do you allow yourself to explore those meaning-of-life thoughts? If the answer is "never," then take time to do that now.

- When do you feel most at peace? Can you allow that sense of God's peace to fill you during other times and during other circumstances?

Prayer

God, I've felt that I've been missing out on life because of one missing piece. Help me to have hope in this area and also to turn my focus toward you and all that you provide. I give you my concerns, my sense of loss, and my hopes...and I will step into your wholeness and abundance.

Afterglow

I will give all areas of my life to God. I'll do that today, tomorrow, and the next day so that it becomes the way I live out my hope.

Freed During the Resistance

*His gifts are free for the taking, but I cannot
take these gifts if my hands are already full
of my own weapons of self-protection.*

KATHERINE WALDEN

I wasn't imprisoned for writing a radical underground newspaper. I didn't plot a rebellion on a college campus. But in my adult life, I've been a part of a resistance. At some point I started to resist the abundant, complete life God was presenting. I said no thanks to travel when staying home sounded more comfortable. I shook my head when the intimidating challenge of trying something new arose without advance notice. I held up my hands to ward off a life trial and then spent the entire span of that trial resisting the lessons it was teaching.

But I can't tell you why. It's funny how you think you know yourself really well but then discover that you've been doing things behind your back. Life-changing things. Like saying no to the life nudged your way over and over again. As I look back at all these paths not taken, these refusals, these excuses that cloud my perception even today…I'm pretty sure I've done more resisting than embracing.

If you can look back on your life and witness a picket line of complaints, excuses, rants, and refusals, then you might be a part of your own resistance. I have wisdom for both of us:

You can't hug something when your arms are folded across your chest in defiance. That sounds a lot like a quip to be attributed to a spunky Southern grandmother, but whatever way you hear it, read it, or take it in is fine by me...as long as you embrace its truth and stop resisting the very lovely life being offered to you.

Shedding Light

- What do you resist the most in your life? Help, love, tenderness, challenge, sadness, growth? Take time to prayerfully figure out why you say no to good things.

- Resistance comes from a place of self-protection. See if you can view each decision and opportunity as a way to peace. Welcome these issues into your life so that you can see how God's peace surpasses our very limited understanding of what is good for us and what can harm us.

Prayer

Just this week I said no to something I was supposed to say yes to without fear and without resistance. God, grant me the seed of hope I need to unfold my arms and to unfold a life of wonder.

Afterglow

I will say yes to more things this week. And I'll accept the good, the bad, the doubts, and the duty tied to each opportunity.

Light a Candle
for Faith

What Are You Looking For?

People see God every day. They just don't recognize him.

PEARL BAILEY

When Jesus came on the scene, he did not meet the list of requirements people had for the Messiah. He spoke as a king might…about the kingdom of God…but he directed his attention to the poor, the diseased, the outcasts. He was smart and wise and well versed in the Jewish law, but he challenged those leaders who represented the law. He spoke with authority and power, yet he showed great humility and mercy. He could command an audience of thousands with his message but he frequently tended to the broken and the lonely one-on-one. Jesus communicated a simple message, of serving God and loving one another, and yet he was a complicated version of who the Messiah was. Jesus shook up established thoughts about religion and faith. He made the message and commitment personal and the call to learn and serve universal.

I'm not surprised people were torn between their religious affiliations and traditions and the appealing, radically different approach of Jesus. Aren't we just as torn today? We might be Christians for many years when suddenly we realize we are so immersed in the world of religion and tradition that we've forgotten how radical the love of Christ is. We feel, with a renewed heart, touched by the call to intimate relationship Jesus places on our hearts.

Do you still expect Jesus to look a certain way? Do you wait for him to act in a commanding, kingly manner rather than through gentle leading and grace? He is powerful and merciful. And he will meet you where you are. He will point out that which is solely religion and that which is wholly faith. He will see your brokenness and talk to you one-on-one. And he will say "follow me." Don't look any further.

Shedding Light

- Do you keep looking for a different version of Jesus? Are you watching for a God who fits your job description for a messiah or are you looking for the real thing? The one who knows your heart and who loves the unlovable?

- Jesus wants to speak to each of us one-on-one. Have you been willing to listen?

Prayer

God, I will set aside my expectations and my demands and my limited perspective of you. Forgive me for accepting only a part of you. Lead me to deeper relationship with the real you. Show me what it is to follow you and to live in the power of grace.

Afterglow

I will stop limiting God with my human perspective so that I can become a seeker of truth and transformation.

Walking Upright

*Trust in the Lord with all your heart
and lean not on your own understanding;
in all your ways acknowledge him,
and he will make your paths straight.*

PROVERBS 3:5-6

Like a lot of women, I slouch my shoulders. When I take inventory of my walk after I get up in the morning, inevitably I find that my shoulders slump inward and I lean forward rather than walk upright. No wonder I am tired much of the day…I start out walking like a woman who carries all her belongings on her back. With concerted effort I'm trying to correct that as I walk around the house or out in the world. Chin down, shoulders back and relaxed, hips aligned with spine, core tightened. It's a lot to keep track of, but I feel better and stronger when I'm walking upright and as tall as a short person is able.

Our walks of faith need similar assessment from time to time. We fall into patterns of movement and adopt habits that compromise our spiritual strength, the integrity of our position about life and love, and our direction. We slouch, we stumble, we lean forward with our own objectives rather than resting back in God's purposes for us. Our decisions, even our intentional spiritual decisions, are made from an off-balance perspective. We end up living lives not aligned with God and his strength.

No wonder we become so tired. No wonder our physical and emotional positioning makes us look like women who carry all of their burdens on their shoulders and their minds.

It is a good day to walk forward, free of those heavy burdens. Did you really want them to begin with? Sharing your load with your Creator is not shirking responsibility; it is your first step toward aligning your steps, choices, decisions, and dreams with his purpose for you.

Shedding Light

- How have your steps detoured from what you believe to be right or true?
- What has been your position while walking in faith? Do you stand strong and walk as one who knows the gifts of grace and purpose?
- As you rest in God, which burden will you lift up to him first?

Prayer

I've noticed how crooked my path has been these past few years. From where I stand, I can barely see the horizon of your purpose, God. Redirect my steps, my posture of faith, my quest for value. I want to know that I'm walking forward with the strength of someone loved, supported, and known by you.

Afterglow

I will focus on how I stand in my faith. As I release each burden to God's care, I'll physically, emotionally, and spiritually feel the difference in my life.

How to Rebuild a Life

*Our real blessings often appear to us
in the shape of pains, losses, and disappointments.*

JOSEPH ADDISON

A few things to know about your breakdown. It isn't pretty to the world. But it is beautiful. It isn't controlled. But it is purposed. It isn't the way you wanted to change your life. But it is the way to freedom. There is a reason the old needs to fall away. The new life requires a beginning built with God's purpose and hope. When God is rebuilding your life and your faith, he will:

- Break down the walls built during past pain to build up the power of forgiveness.

- Break down the coldness of religiosity to build up the intimacy of personal faith.

- Break down the stereotype of success to build up the truth of abundant living.

- Break down the need for control to build up your readiness for divine guidance.

- Break down the expectations you've built up to build up your hope for the promises of God.

Our transformation is taking place when we watch life as we've known it crumble around the edges and sink into the faulty foundation of anger, pain, regret, and emptiness. It might look like loss, but it is the image of gaining abundance. It might feel like starting over, but it is really about moving forward. Faith wasn't built in a day. Okay, I borrowed part of that line from something else, but it's still true. Things that last aren't built overnight. We can receive salvation in an instant, but faith is ongoing and evolving because it is a relationship with a living God. Those times of tearing down will lead to the rebuilding and restoration of your faith and your life. Don't try to salvage the ruins. Spend time with *the* Architect and celebrate the new plans that are unfolding.

Shedding Light

- The word "blessing" is thrown around a lot. What does it mean to you?

- Can you view a recent loss or struggle as a blessing? Do you see how your deconstruction is leading to the rebuilding of faith and hope?

- The new thing God is creating in your life will lead you forward. Trust in that.

Prayer

God, as much as I want to rest in the blessings of this trial, I'm not there yet. Today, can I just rest in your shelter? I look forward to the restoration I know will come. Your faithfulness in the past builds up my faith today, and I am grateful.

Afterglow

I will stop building walls so that I can see the life being rebuilt by God's compassion and peace.

It's Personal

*All I have seen teaches me
to trust the Creator for all I have not seen.*

RALPH WALDO EMERSON

How did you come to faith? What was it that beckoned you to belief? During my years of interacting with others who profess similar beliefs, I've noticed that we each have our own personal understanding and tenderness toward our faith. Often it is directly related to whichever wonder, truth, or gift that revealed God's presence to us in the first place.

So what led you to that moment of faith? What caught your attention in the middle of a hardship or a season of busyness? What made your heart stir with that sense of home and belonging that God's presence provides? Was it the:

- Perspective of the eternal in light of life's frailty
- Gift of salvation
- Surprise and comfort of God's love
- Unexpected mercy
- Intimacy with and accessibility to God
- Wisdom of the Bible
- Manifestations of faith in someone else's life
- Transforming power of grace
- Tenderness and profundity of Jesus
- Miracle of resurrection

Was your invitation to faith through an encounter with Christ when you were actively searching—or when you were going about your own business and not giving the Creator much thought? God is full of surprises. Maybe it took a time of extreme loneliness or dissatisfaction before you recognized that God's art is wholeness. It is good to recognize how we have come to this place of faith. Be grateful for your journey. Be thankful for the faith journeys of others. You and I...we are blessed with distinct gifts and purpose; it shouldn't be a surprise that he calls us to his heart in very unique, personal ways. That's how God works. You've heard...in mysterious ways.

Shedding Light

- How were you called to faith? Is it hard for you to relate to people who came to faith for different reasons?
- Are you still observing rather than residing in belief? What fears or reservations do you have?
- Try to see God's art of wholeness in others. We all bear the Creator's signature.

Prayer

God, I'm so grateful for this journey. I've been through many things since I first believed in you and felt that sense of home and belonging. Thank you for your faithfulness, even during my times of uncertainty.

Afterglow

I'll reflect on how I came to faith, and I'll celebrate all that this path of belief offers me personally.

Believing in Others

There are different kinds of gifts, but the same Spirit.
There are different kinds of service, but the same Lord.
There are different kinds of working, but the
same God works all of them in all men.

1 CORINTHIANS 12:4-6

Reliance on God is an important part of faith. Reliance on how God works in the hearts and lives of others is equally important. I'm always amazed by the goodness and selflessness that people demonstrate. They donate time and money to local charity organizations, contribute to vital causes across the globe, stand up for the rights of people they will never meet, pray for and serve the needs of acquaintances and strangers, and respond to God's leading.

All of God's children are made in his image. Some might not know him intimately yet or believe that he can move through them toward a personal purpose, but God still leads, changes hearts, convicts the spirit, inspires transformation.

Our dependence on God should not put us at risk of becoming completely independent of others. Have you ever needed support desperately but wouldn't trust others to step up, so you didn't even ask? Or have you requested help and expected nobody to follow through...and been pleasantly surprised? Have faith in others. Watch for their goodness and their good works. Every day there will be instances that remind you of the faithfulness of the heart formed by God and for God. Don't underestimate the courage and compassion of the person next door, the man looking for work, the woman at the checkout counter.

Presume the best about people, and you will discover the very best of humanity. If we commit to this perspective, we will discover the greater thing indeed…why and how "God so loved the world."

Shedding Light

- When have you been surprised by an individual's response to a need or to a community's outpouring of kindness?

- How do you respond to needs you see around you? Are you depending on God to have other people step up while you hold back out of fear or lack of motivation?

- Allow yourself to be amazed by compassion. Ask for help. Believe in the faithfulness of others.

Prayer

I am not always quick to believe in others. I want them to prove themselves. Guide my heart away from fear so that I can open my eyes to the faithfulness of others. I want to see you in the goodness that is around me in friends and strangers.

Afterglow

I'll believe in the people I encounter today. I will look for and see the beauty of their potential and their heart.

Life with a View

*Life without faith in something is
too narrow a space to live.*

GEORGE LANCASTER SPALDING

After much prayer, a middle-aged woman decided to take a long-delayed trip to a foreign city. She arrived at her hotel filled with excitement. She told the manager that this trip was answered prayer. His face turned red. "We've misplaced your reservation. Please have a seat while I fix this. I'm so sorry."

"I'm not worried. Whatever room you have is fine. But…a view would be so special."

Ten minutes later the manager asked the woman to follow him. They took the elevator to the nineteenth floor. "I think you'll like this view," he said with a broad smile. The woman entered what was clearly the penthouse suite. The manager pointed out the amenities to her, but her eyes were fixed on the glass double doors which framed a breathtaking view of the city square and an exquisite park.

Every morning, the woman sipped coffee on the terrace and planned her outings. She spent evenings full of gratitude looking at the glow of lampposts in the park. On her last evening, she ordered room service so she could savor her beloved view.

The manager himself delivered the meal and asked if she would like him to start a fire in the fireplace. She pulled her glance away from the window and looked at him. "What fire-place?" she asked. He furrowed his brow, took three steps back, and opened up a set of double doors, revealing a large living area of velvet furniture and a marble mantel fireplace.

"Oh, my! I thought those doors led to another closet!"

The manager, clearly appalled, stammered for several seconds and then said, "It's so terrible! Here you are in the penthouse, on your dream trip, and you didn't get to enjoy the riches of it."

The woman laughed, turned back to the window, and sighed. "Oh, yes I did."

Shedding Light

- Are you savoring the riches of your life?

- When one of your dreams is realized, are you quick to see how it is flawed or not quite the way you imagined? Or do you focus on the beauty of the moment and the riches of a new life experience?

- Do you cherish the gifts God provides? Big, small, ordinary, miraculous?

Prayer

What have I been doing all this time? Some dreams I have put off, others I have ruined by picking them apart when they don't fit my vision of perfection. God, help me to embrace this life of mine…I don't want to miss a moment.

Afterglow

I will live richly and abundantly by savoring the view of my life.

Light a Candle
for Healing

Beauty of Resurrection

*Often, in the midst of great problems, we
stop short of the real blessing God has for us,
which is a fresh vision of who He is.*

ANNE GRAHAM LOTZ

There was a time when things changed for you and me. When losses left gaps in our dreams and swayed our paths with such force that we never quite got back on track. Many of us have spent a lifetime trying to retrieve what went missing so long ago. Whatever we have lost through mistakes, brokenness, pain, illness, or rejection leaves us with a picture of "what could have been" had those sufferings never occurred. Retrieval involves a constant desire to re-create what we had just before things shifted. Just before we lost our way. Just before we reluctantly changed our plans and dreams.

Don't confuse the human instinct of retrieval with the divine intention of resurrection. Retrieval works double-time to reestablish what was. It is a painstaking, detailed effort to put everything back in its place just so. But resurrection is God's life-giving force. It doesn't strive to repeat life because that would take away from the power that loss can bring when we understand its nature. Resurrection seeks to find what *will* be—what *can* be—because of a void, a hunger, a sorrow. It doesn't try to piece together a shabby version of an old life because it is designed to nurture, create, and establish something new. It uses the materials found in the aftermath of loss, but it never tries to return to life before that loss. There isn't power in those remnants you hold in your hand so tightly. Grab onto the life that is being created in you now. You have a new vision of life and a truer understanding of God's love and care. Beautiful and meaningful things can come of loss if we don't try to re-create something old, but prepare ourselves to embrace a new life.

Shedding Light

- Have you invested more belief in retrieval than in resurrection?

- Do you want something that replicates the past or something that transcends what is known and offers rebirth? How can you move toward the latter?

- The life lived in the power of Christ's resurrection doesn't mourn the small deaths of circumstances and seasons. This is a life that sees beginnings and restoration with each change.

Prayer

I really want to live in the power of the resurrection, Lord. I believe in transformation and a life renewed and changed by your grace. When I try to control that power by seeking to retrieve something lost, I will let go so that I can experience what can unfold through your grace.

Afterglow

I'll release my hold on those remnants of past dreams or broken paths and will reach out for the beauty of a new vision, a new truth.

Today Is for Living

Trust the past to God's mercy, the present to God's love, and the future to God's providence.

AUGUSTINE

If I were to ask you to describe your past failings and regrets, would your response be so vivid, detailed, and clear that the truth would be known—these regrets are not at all in your past but are very much in your present? Do you keep such things alive by giving them time and meditation, both of which are gifts you could be giving to God?

It's time to discard past mistakes and let yesterday do the job it was made for. Yesterday is our wise teacher when we glean its many lessons. Yesterday is our testimony when we can share about our transformation through faith and God's love. Yesterday is our reminder that God can lead us through loss and error and pride and pain. But yesterday is not our substitution for today.

If your regrets are alive and kicking, it's because you are fueling them with current thoughts and nurturing them with the oxygen and space of your present. Do you need help carrying those regrets to the foot of the cross? Are you ready to leave them for dead—because the power of the resurrection does not exist so that you can resurrect your mistakes and tend to them; it exists so that you can live abundantly in the present and have hope for a future. God's mercy has covered those difficulties and mistakes so that you can be alive in the moment and be used for greater purposes than being a life-support machine for your past. You decide each and every morning what you are going to give your presence and passions over to...the unchangeable past or the abundant and transforming present.

Shedding Light

- Which regrets do you nurture and keep alive? Are you prepared to give those up for something better?

- Old wounds can reopen time after time. I think we can become addicted to the pain and the drama. Let them truly heal so that they are a source of wisdom only.

Prayer

I'm so glad to have moved on in my life. I don't want my past failings to become my focus today. There is so much more to experience in this moment and in the future because of you. Redirect my thoughts and my sense of direction...lead me away from yesterday. It has done its job.

Afterglow

I will make sure my regrets are not being nourished by my actions and thoughts today. I'll only give energy and effort to today's hope.

Where Does It Hurt?

Let God's promises shine on your problems.

CORRIE TEN BOOM

We've come through a lot. We've faced hardships and surprises and times of need. When we've gone through an extreme difficulty and our lives seem fragmented by the cuts of sorrow, healing comes to us in different ways. Our ideas of what healing will look like and what it will free us to do once our damaged area has been repaired are so limited that we are likely to miss out on the restoration we receive.

Our healing might be taking place in a different area than the one so blatantly marked by our pain. If you've prayed for restoration in a relationship, your healing might come in the form of a new perspective about that relationship. You might need to labor through the healing and then be willing to see things anew on the other side of it. "Fix me" or "fix this" might be our heart's cry, but "one remedy suits all" is not usually how God's healing manifests in our circumstances. God is very personal in his interaction with us and how he soothes, comforts, and leads his children. Our pleas represent where we are emotionally, and often at our crisis point. And his promises are true and far reaching in our lives.

God sees our lives from beginning to end. From joy to sorrow to joy again. From need to abundance. His balm reaches the places within us we might not know are broken. So, our desire for physical healing might be met with physical healing, but be prepared to recognize the healing of an emotional wound that has long needed the balm of God's peace.

Shedding Light

- Where do you hurt? Ask God to shine light on the source of those hurts.
- Have you given thanks for past times of healing? It is important to acknowledge God's continuous work in your life. It helps you to recognize his healing in all circumstances.

Prayer

Comfort me, God. I want to have my pain soothed and my hurts healed. Prepare my heart to see and accept the way that healing is manifested in my life. Thank you for the balm of your peace and love.

Afterglow

I will share the joy of my healing with others. I will make known the goodness of redemption.

Healing After the Healing

*Birds sing after a storm; why shouldn't people feel
as free to delight in whatever remains to them?*

ROSE FITZGERALD KENNEDY

I've had the opportunity to lift up prayers for healing on behalf
of someone I love. And together we've witnessed and experienced healing. We approach God with hearts full of gratitude
for the gifts of well-being, hope, and recovery. But life doesn't
look the way we thought it would. So how do we carry the
hope of healing into this new experience?

Just as we don't always recognize the way healing has manifested in our bodies, relationships, hearts, and beliefs, we don't
always recognize the post-healing life as the one we are intended
to live out with conviction and peace. Because we are looking
for a return to the life we once had, we often don't recognize
the revised version of life we are given instead. Healing does
not drag us back to time before the hardship; it moves us forward in knowledge, peace, and intimacy with God. This season
may come with limitations and difficulties. Pressing on in this
new version of life is still part of your healing. As tough as it
can be, it is nevertheless a gift to see your life with new eyes, to
walk with strength and appreciation toward different goals, to
modify your expectations and begin living abundantly in your
purpose rather than in your preconceived notions.

Loss and suffering and times of paralyzing disbelief change us from within. We do not come out the other side as the same person who went in to the trial. You are now living as a person who has been touched by transformation, renewal, and grace. Embrace the newness of healing.

Shedding Light

- Are you on the other side of a trial and still trying to make sense of how your life is now? How is it different? How is it the same?

- Can you let go of how you thought life would be after healing? God knows your life's big picture while you only experience a peephole version of it. Step forward into this healing.

- Does disbelief creep into your thoughts and prayers? Allow grace to cover your doubt.

Prayer

I'm trusting your healing, God. I welcome it and will walk forward in it. Remove those expectations I've placed on what life will be or should be. Open my heart to the wonder of your hope for me personally.

Afterglow

I won't watch for the human version of perfection, but will seek the healing that comes from the Perfector of my faith.

Gold for Sorrow

Be truly glad. There is wonderful joy ahead, even
though you have to endure many trials for a little while.
These trials will show that your faith is genuine. It
is being tested as fire tests and purifies gold—though
your faith is far more precious than mere gold.

1 PETER 1:6-7 NLT

Someone once told me that in cases of extreme grief, a gold compound has been given to patients as part of homeopathic treatment. I found that fascinating. I realize the doctor didn't say "swallow two class rings and call me in the morning." Nevertheless, I still found the concept of a precious metal used as medicine to be fascinating and poetically appropriate. Like gold, our lives can be put through the fires. The flames that touch and refine our faith are those of suffering and grief.

During our most personal and overwhelming trials, we have the gift of faith. We can lean into our faith and find rest. We can step under the covering of our faith in God for refuge. As the verse above illuminates, our faith is more precious than gold...especially for our healing. Our hope in God's peace and purpose carries us during seasons of sorrow.

When someone you care about is facing the shock of grief, it is through faith that you can be a source of strength and comfort. You can be a companion for their journey by being

---

prayerful, tender, and generous. Your presence might encourage them to enter God's presence, where they'll experience mercy far surpassing human compassion.

As sojourners of faith, we have something else that leads us to hope and healing: "The laws of the Lord are true; each one is fair. They are more desirable than gold, even the finest gold" (Psalm 19:9-10 NLT). Try as we might, we cannot fully comprehend the mysteries of life and death, but we can cherish the pursuit of God's truth. We can desire, even in our sorrow, the beauty of a wound healed and the sacredness of a faith refined.

Shedding Light

- How has your faith been refined through the fire of trials or disappointments?

- Exchange your sorrow for God's healing. You'll get a great return on it!

- Would others in your life know the value of God's mercy? Be compassionate so that they feel the hope of healing.

Prayer

God, your comfort sustains me. You hold me up when I want to sink into grief. The refuge you provide is one that is hard for me to explain to others, and yet I hold onto it with absolute faith. You are with me in joy and in sorrow. There is nothing of greater value than your love.

Afterglow

God's truth will be my measure of what is priceless and beautiful in this season and in the future.

First Thoughts

Suffering is more or less inevitable in life, but it's not redemptive unless we allow God to make good use of it.

MOLLY WOLF

I waited for word about my husband after his surgery. It seemed forever before I could see him. By the time I did, he had surfaced from the cloud of anesthesia. He was groggy but very aware. I held his hand, kissed him, and asked him how he felt. Instead of talking about his physical state, he asked if we could pray for a guy a few curtained areas over. We couldn't see the man, but we could hear him cry out. While the staff in the overflow ICU area did all they could to ease this man's pain, we prayed for his healing and recovery.

This wasn't the first time my husband's waking thoughts were about someone else. On another occasion he prayed for a young man who had caused quite a ruckus because he wanted a cigarette before his surgery. While these loud and illogical demands had been a bit entertaining initially, we both knew that the boy was scared to undergo a serious operation. I love that my husband's initial impulse after going through his own ordeal was to seek the comfort of prayer for someone else. My husband isn't a saint, but he is kind and sensitive. His pain has led him to be more prayerful and perceptive regarding the needs of others.

When we face hardships of any kind, we might be tempted to shut down our hope and shut off those first thoughts of God's mercy. But our personal healing is possible when we are able to recognize and care about the pain of others. No matter what burdens we are dealing with, let our first thoughts each morning be of those we can lift up to God. Let's experience the healing of compassion.

Shedding Light

- Who needs thoughts and prayers of compassion? Your neighbor, a parent, a friend?

- If you are so busy that you rarely lift up your own concerns, what will it take to become quiet and still enough to pray for others?

- How have your past struggles made you more sensitive to those around you?

Prayer

God, give me a genuine heart for the needs of others. Direct my first thoughts after waking or after my trials to be of compassion. I love the idea of turning my times of pain into a greater inclination toward peace. May I draw on my own healing journey for strength and sensitivity.

Afterglow

Before I pray for myself, I will pray for others.

Light a
Candle for Joy

Inviting Joy

Don't think so much about who is for or
against you, rather give all your care, that
God be with you in everything you do.

Thomas á Kempis

Build a life with what you have and joy will follow. Our
worries tend to center on what won't happen, so much so
that we miss out on celebrating what will and does happen. A
friend was planning a lovely family gathering. Days in advance,
she made preparations for those who would be coming, but
her thoughts turned to those who might not show up and why.
She knew their presence would be missed and so she continued
to dwell on them. Soon she was no longer enjoying the process
of preparation; her heart had changed focus. Then her husband
pointed out a great perspective: When the day comes for the
gathering, the ones who show up are the ones to take care of.

How easy it can be to be surrounded by people we care
about and still not emotionally be with them because we are
preoccupied with the scenario that will not be, at least not this
time. If people stopped offering up themselves and their passions until they had the ultimate turnout or the perfect group,
then the careers of most musicians would end after one hotel
lounge performance. Grassroots organizations would dry up
before the mission statement could be read to those who would

benefit from its intention. And most ministries would fizzle out after one poorly attended Wednesday night meeting.

If we consider that each gathering is an opportunity of community and connection, then there isn't any good reason to fret over who isn't there. Celebrate and tend to those God brings to you and those God encourages you to join with. At your next gathering, meeting, event, or stuck-elevator incident, look around at the people you are meant to interact with and get to know. Joy is among them.

Shedding Light

- Do you focus more on what might not happen than you do on following through with your role?

- Have you pulled back from your purpose because it wasn't unfolding the way you wanted it to?

- Serve those who do show up in your life. Friends and strangers alike…they are there for a reason, and you're called to show up as well.

Prayer

Give me a heart for what does happen and for each person I meet, Lord. When I want to change plans just because things aren't turning out the way I had planned, give me a new vision and passion for what is unfolding. I will invite faith and joy to be a part of every circumstance and opportunity.

Afterglow

I will be there for others, I will invite joy, and I will be grateful for all who show up in my life.

Sabbath for Breakfast

What I do today is important because I am
exchanging a day of my life for it.

HUGH MULLIGAN

My quest for a good breakfast turned into a morning of simple joys. I zipped up my lightweight vest and tied a scarf around my neck as I stepped out into the cool morning. I leapt over curbside puddles and continued at a quick clip, eager for hash browns and eggs and a big coffee. Strange weather patterns this season left unlikely impressions everywhere. Yellow and purple-red fall leaves were encased in the thin layer of midwinter ice on sidewalks. I was about to lean down and salvage one when I became distracted by the woman ahead of me who juggled a briefcase and a coffee. Actually it was her pants' very wet hem that caught my attention and made me mindful of the fate of my own jeans. When a kind motorist stopped to let me cross the street, I gathered fabric at my knee to hike up my pant leg and sauntered to the other side. I felt like a Victorian woman gathering the folds of her silk skirt to make her way past a carriage.

My first restaurant choice, so nonestablishment that it's established as a town favorite, was packed. I kept walking. The second breakfast place, casual and filled with neighborhood regulars, was also overflowing. An older couple read the morning paper outside the café door. It would be a while. My feet kept moving, and I ended up at a park several blocks past my usual routes. Moms pushed strollers, young couples held gloved hands, squirrels made fast tracks through the lawn. With a quick stop at a corner establishment, I had a large coffee in my hands and kept on walking…taking in the morning. My cheeks stung from the cold and my body was invigorated from the walk.

So what if I didn't get the breakfast I was craving. It was all worth it. I highly recommend letting go of your agenda and getting lost in a morning of delicious pleasures.

Shedding Light

- Create your own Sabbath morning or day. Give rest, joy, and delight a place in your life.

- Set aside a time each day to reflect on what brings pleasure and meaning to your existence. Find ways to nurture those activities.

- Notice your life and all of its treasures. There are many. Each day is remarkable!

Prayer

Why do I let week after week go by without spending time honoring life? I live it, but I don't celebrate it. Today is a gift. Thank you, Lord, for the smallest of treasures that I uncover. Show me how to feel my life deeply.

Afterglow

I will head out today with one main goal: to breathe joy into my life and to delight in God's gifts.

Joy Harvest

*It is within my power either to serve God or not
to serve him. Serving him, I add to my own good
and the good of the whole world. Not serving him,
I forfeit my own good and deprive the world of
that good, which was in my power to create.*

LEO TOLSTOY

You can tell much about a life by what it produces, by what
comes forth into the world from that life's effort and existence. The work of our hands and hearts are often compared
to harvests in the Bible. I consider the produce of our lives to
be a matter of faith and faith alone. What pours forth from our
efforts, love, and decisions reflects what is going on in our hearts.
When we produce crops of complaints, arguments, destructive
language and actions, self-hatred, and anger, our hearts are distant from God's leading and we've stopped tapping into God's
unconditional love as our source for life.

Athenagoras, a philosopher and Christian apologist in the
latter part of the second century, described the Holy Spirit as
an effluence of God. That struck me as a very lovely and profound explanation. The Holy Spirit flows out of God. It makes
sense to me that the outpouring of God is the Spirit. They are
one, and they are separate. Ah, the confounding mystery of the
Trinity. But we're not going there; we're going to your heart. If

---

God is your center, goodness and joy should be the effluence of your soul, your speech, your thoughts, and your intentions. Does love and abundance flow from your faith? What else does your faith produce? Is there gladness, passion for dreams, deep empathy for those in pain, a hunger for justice, and an abiding love for God and God's children?

During your time of reflection, consider what is flowing from your life. Do you emanate a peace that is of God? Instead of trying to have influence with power, money, or emotional leverage, wouldn't we offer the world much more healing and joy if we desire to be an effluence of faith?

Shedding Light

- What flows from your life now? What would you like to be the effluence of your daily living?

- The joy of a harvest is that there is abundance to share. Give of whatever God produces in your life.

- Seek the leading of the Holy Spirit so that your actions today are of God.

Prayer

Show me how to love with your love, God. Show me how to be joyful and generous with the bounty of faith you give to me daily. May I never hold back a portion of your goodness so that others receive these offerings freely.

Afterglow

I will be mindful and prayerful today so that the harvest of my efforts and actions are goodness, joy, peace, and kindness.

One, Two, Cha Cha Cha

Life is either a daring adventure or nothing.

HELEN KELLER

Maneuvering life is hard. Learning to take the right steps and make the correct moves can trip us up at any point. Even when I thought I had memorized good instruction, I've jammed my big toe, and I've leapt when I should have bowed. I have always been a closet learner, wanting to master something on my own, away from possible evaluation and scrutiny. Do you prefer to carefully orchestrate how you learn, when you learn, and when you feel ready enough to try something under the gaze of another? The shocking and embarrassing truth is that most of the time nobody is watching. But if we focus on ourselves long enough, we don't notice that no one is noticing. It isn't that people don't care; they just happen to have better things to do. Or maybe they are focused on themselves and not the woman trying to knit in public for the first time or the person working up the courage to dine alone at the corner bistro.

We command joy out of our lives when we place ourselves in charge of the learning curve. When we say no to opportunities that take us by surprise, we miss out on God's leading. You aren't the designer of your life. You make choices, and you can refuse to open up to possible failure and public ridicule, but you have to release control to God. When you or I limit the number of times we're willing to try, we're also placing a limit on how often we'll trust God. Where's the joy in that life?

We should learn something together. Let's take up something daring like juggling fire, kayaking level-5 rapids, or maybe something as radical as doing a basic, unpracticed dance move in public. That first demonstration of faith and freedom could lead us to some amazing next steps.

Shedding Light

- What have you been putting off for years because you haven't wanted to risk failure?

- Build up the courage of a friend today by encouraging their dreams and opportunities.

- Risk your heart a little, risk your pride a lot…move forward in ways that serve your spirit of joy and also in ways that serve others somehow.

Prayer

God, I claim to have faith, and yet I hold back from walking in that faith. Where is my trust in your support and your leading? Give me courage. Help me break through my hesitation, excuses, and pride to see the joy in taking leaps of faith and delighting in a life without limits.

Afterglow

I'm stepping out today and trying something new with courage and faith, focused on the joy of the activity and not on my predicted outcome.

Light Therapy

*For light I go directly to the Source of
light, not to any of the reflections.*

PEACE PILGRIM

When you are light deprived, your body hungers for light. I live in a region that has some very pleasant months but also has a very long rainy season. It's easy for moods to follow the way of weather patterns, so my husband and I bought a special blue light that is supposed to emulate sunshine and produce similar good effects in the body and mind. All that is required? You sit with the gentle blue rays beaming in your direction for 15 to 30 minutes each morning. What a worthwhile trade-off for an improved mood and better sleep.

Our spirits need light too. We crave the warmth of God's light. It offers nourishment and comfort. It fills us with hope and energy to press on. Imagine how much better our lives will be when we make a commitment to spend 15 minutes a day basking in God's light. It will improve our demeanor, outlook, attitude, perspective, motives, heart, and our sense of joy.

Do you take time to let the light in? Are you in actual spiritual darkness, spending your days under the cloud of depression, sadness, loneliness? I believe many of us and many of the people in our lives are experiencing the negative side effects of insufficient illumination. We need the radiance of promises, hope, and love. How do we seek the Source? Explore Scripture verses that speak to your needs right now. Light your candle and close your eyes and pray. Not sure what to say? Ask for joy. Ask to become a reflection of God's brilliance. Discover how to radiate the love that is given to you from God every day (well beyond a 15-minute session).

No need to flip a switch. Just turn over a new leaf, perhaps. Today is the day you can seek God's light and experience the lasting joy of everlasting love.

Shedding Light

- Have you lost the luster of a vibrant faith? Have you become dull in mind and spirit? When your thoughts are self-focused and every day is the same because you distance yourself from the spark of inspiration, you are ready for light therapy.

- For best results, place God's light at heart level. Studying about God is good, but to embrace the joy of Christ you need to direct the light of God's love at your heart. Be filled by the promises of transformation and grace. From your heart, God will illuminate the way of his will and his hope for you.

Prayer

How have I lived in such darkness for so long, God? I want the light back in my life.

Afterglow

I'll go to the light of God today to refuel, restore, and renew my sense of joy.

Ha-Ha Moment

When unhappy, one doubts everything;
when happy, one doubts nothing.

JOSEPH ROUX

Where does your happiness come from? Do you have any? Is it a quality you lack and wish you had? I've always been a bit envious of people who are quick to laugh and who find something funny at every turn. I've never been one of those people. I enjoy great humor and people who can make me laugh, but I don't start conversations with "have you heard the one about…" and I never will.

What about you? Do the demands of adulthood leave you serious and uptight? When you look toward the future, are you tense with the stress of what might happen? Happiness is a funny thing (how appropriate). It might exist in the future, but it can only be felt and experienced in the here and now. Worry seems to have a devastatingly long shelf life. That's why it's so easy to stockpile it. But happiness needs nurturing, refreshment, and the source of lasting joy—God.

Happiness and joy are not one and the same. Joy is the gift that allows you to see the silver lining of a difficult circumstance. Joy lifts you up even as responsibility and pressure might weigh you down. Joy is the catalyst for happiness. Some people operate in happy mode, but when struggles come, they don't have a foundation of joy to tap into. They need something to spark that ha-ha moment. Do you know people who are jokesters? Ha-ha moments that boost our spirits and offer us a burst of delight are fabulous (bring them on), but they *will* come and go, and our emotions can take the roller-coaster ride right along with them. But the joy of the Lord is continuous, lasting, consistent, ever-present, and, without a doubt, good for the soul.

Shedding Light

- Are you a bowl of laughs until the party is over? Keep the happiness flowing by tapping into the joy of God's love and creativity.

- When have you relied on God during a trial? Were there surprising moments of joy during a time of sorrow? Joy and sorrow can coexist when we turn to God's goodness and mercy during a season of perseverance or a moment of pain.

Prayer

I'm looking for a little levity, Lord. Help me to see the way through my trials with a heart that bursts with your love. You turn my weariness into awareness so that I can see the joy of a new day, the beauty of another person's gifts, the hope of a future, and the promise of wholeness. I am grateful.

Afterglow

I will light my candle and think of ways to build up my foundation of joy. I will rest in God's faithfulness, and I will see ha-ha moments as a gift and lasting joy as the fruit of my spiritual life.

*Light a Candle
for Compassion*

Mercy, Mercy Me

*The wisdom that is from above is first pure,
then peaceable, gentle, willing to yield, full of
mercy and good fruits, without partiality and
without hypocrisy. Now the fruit of righteousness
is sown in peace by those who make peace.*

JAMES 3:17-18 NKJV

For such a gentle word, mercy is a courageous and transforming act when it is bestowed and experienced. True mercy is
given by one who has power over the one who needs forgiveness.
A judge grants mercy to an offender of the law. God is merciful toward his broken children. In daily life we have opportunities to offer mercy to others, and such an opportunity often
involves allowing a "gotcha" moment to pass on by. Mercy very
well might require that you swallow your own pride.

Rather than lord our power or influence over a friend or
loved one, we can express compassion. If you're struggling to
remember a time when you felt that you had any power at all,
you might be looking for the wrong kind of power. We do have
strength. We are placed in situations when we can and should
forgive another. If a visiting child breaks a family heirloom,
you have an opportunity for mercy. When a waitress spills hot
coffee onto your hand instead of into your mug, you can show
mercy. If a driver edges into your lane because they made a

last-minute decision to exit, you are gifted with a mercy moment. The day a friend returns a borrowed, dry-clean-only sweater that is now shrunken and tiny, try mercy on for size.

I didn't say mercy was easy. I said it was gentle, courageous, and transforming. Share your new understanding of mercy when you are placed as judge or teacher or parent of another. Your mercy will generate the gift of peace for yourself and others.

Shedding Light

- When have you shown great mercy? When have you not shown compassion for another and regretted it later?

- Train your heart and mind on God's love so that mercy becomes your nature.

- If you enjoy or desire having power over someone else at work or at home, step back and give that situation to God in prayer. Chances are you'll need a pride adjustment.

Prayer

My fuse seems to be so short lately. God, grant me a heart that expresses real compassion. I know the truest, deepest, most transforming compassion because of your grace. Help me to pass it on...especially when my pride wants me to correct, limit, or judge another.

Afterglow

I'll extend grace and mercy to everyone I meet today.

Called to Immediate Action

I have found that among its other benefits,
giving liberates the soul of the giver.

Maya Angelou

Vivid documentaries of famine and poverty can move us to tears and compel us to send money to a cause based in a country we've never even visited. These are good impulses. But where many of us struggle with compassion is in our own circles, our own towns, and our community centers. The close proximity of poverty and pain can make us uncomfortable, even as our hearts ache for the need we see in our immediate areas. Spreading love and our resources to the ends of the earth is a good use of our time and our priorities, but we cannot do that and neglect sharing God's love with those closest to us.

Being a physical representative of Christ's love for another is a powerful act. When we first reach out to another person and touch their shoulder and look them in the eyes and express compassion, we will understand the importance of this personal, intimate connection with God's children. What does it look like to be Christ's hands? We are his hands and his heart when we are serving meals, reading mail to an elderly neighbor, giving someone money without conditions, offering to cook meals for a friend who is ill, holding hands with a person in the hospital, or listening to the needs and the life story of a stranger.

This isn't an easy or comfortable step for a lot of us. So we can pray and we can start by noticing the hearts and aches of the people in our own home. Then those of our neighbors. Then we can expand our awareness to the people we cross paths with on our way to work or at the bus stop. Loving those close to home with the unconditional love of Christ can change the world.

Shedding Light

- When you ask to see the needs and hurts of others… you will. Prepare to be prayerful and to draw from God's compassion.

- Have you wept for the heartache of another? Don't hold back from empathy. It connects you to the brokenness of others and then back to your own brokenness. Ultimately, it leads you right back to God's heart.

- Consider ways to be the hands of Christ. Preaching the gospel is for some…living the gospel is for all of us.

Prayer

God, where are those needs? I'm ready to see them and to respond to them. Even the people closest to me are good at hiding their pain and ignoring their need. Show me how to be vulnerable so that they are invited to do the same in my presence and in yours.

Afterglow

I won't turn away from those who are hurting, but I will reach out and make a connection.

One Car Over

*We can choose to obey the still small stirring
within, the little whisper that says, "Go. Ask.
Reach out. Be an answer to someone's plea. You
have a part to play. Have faith." We can decide
to risk that He is indeed there, watching, caring,
cherishing us as we love and accept love.*

JOAN WESTER ANDERSON

If you spend a few moments wondering who in your life might need prayer and are at a loss for someone to lift up, I think either the people in your life are experiencing amazingly good fortune or you are limiting your sense of neighbor too greatly. Could it very well be the latter? In our transitory society, our definition of neighbor should also be transitory. We can include those people we stand by at the post office or walk by on the way to our metro stop. We should include those who provide our mail, pick up our recycling, or deliver our favorite croissants to the corner coffee shop.

For me, it's good to ease into a spiritual philosophy shift slowly. I've started by considering the person or people one car over. It could contain anyone. A two-year-old having a meltdown in the backseat. A college student thumping their fingers on the steering wheel to the beat of a song while contemplating his purpose in life. A mother having a meltdown in the driver's seat. A woman heartbroken over the loss of her father. A father heartsick because this car has been his family's home since he lost his job last month. One car over is someone who needs prayer. Not because their life is a mess or on the brink of disaster, but because we all need prayer. We all need people to look at us through the compassionate eyes of a true neighbor.

Think differently and feel differently about the people who cross your route, even if just for the duration of a stoplight.

Shedding Light

- Who have you avoided becoming "neighbors" with? Reach out in a small way next time you have the chance.

- Prepare your heart to be more compassionate during your day. Spend moments in prayer in the morning. Read Scripture. Ask God to present you with the people who need a neighbor's awareness and kindness.

Prayer

That person next to me...here at the busy intersection...they cut me off three blocks ago. I don't know what they need, but you do. Cover them, guide them, give them a sense of peace today that steadies their heart and gives them a glimpse of hope.

Afterglow

I'll consider myself connected, responsible, and tied to others through compassion.

Jesus Loves Me

We are called to love the world. And God loved the world so much that He gave Jesus. Today He loves the world so much that He gives you and me to be His love, His compassion, and His presence, through a life of prayer, of sacrifice, of surrender to God.

MOTHER TERESA

The song "Jesus Loves Me" is a sweet tune that children learn in Sunday school, and yet its simple and radical truth can fill any adult with deep emotion. Oh, what it is to be loved so completely and so gently. This personal intimacy with God is one shared between all of God's children and their Creator. For some of us it is easy and logical to jump wholly and completely into the arms of the Divine. For others of us, it takes a longer time to be able to say "Jesus loves me" and to believe it on a soul level. But no matter when the truth of God's love does sink in, that great love envelops the heart and manifests in significant ways. Forgiveness in human relationships has new meaning. Connections to others are strengthened. The load of burdens is lessened. A sense of individual purpose replaces a random pursuit of success.

I take for granted the power of knowing that Jesus loves me, even though I rest in the comfort of that knowledge daily and cannot imagine life without that understanding. I know I am taking it for granted when I don't share it. The result of believing "Jesus loves me" should be visible fruits of service, generosity, grace, and mercy. When our hearts feel the compassion of Christ over and over, we know to go to God's reserve of patience and insight to keep on caring.

Knowing that Jesus loves me is my impetus to seek fellowship in this world even when it is awkward, hard, or uncomfortable. "Jesus loves me" is the powerful precursor to "Jesus loves you."

Shedding Light

- Has your head and heart knowledge of Jesus' love transformed the way you love others?
- What are some practical ways to say "Jesus loves you" to people you meet?
- Have you exchanged the pursuit of success for the pursuit of purpose?

Prayer

Lead me to transformed love, Lord. I come to you for patience and the strength to care for others. When I weigh the potential burden of helping another or supporting them in their time of need, remind me of the burdens you have taken from me. May I use my freedom to lead others to the same.

Afterglow

I will take the risk of deeper communion with a person in my life.

I Wish I Knew

When you get into a tight place and everything goes
against you, till it seems as though you could not
hang on a minute longer, never give up then, for that
is just the place and time that the tide will turn.

HARRIET BEECHER STOWE

I wish I knew what kept you up late staring at the dark while chasing shadows in your mind. You're dealing with stresses others aren't even aware of, and yet you keep a brave face until you are out of public viewing and in the solitude of nightfall. You're being brave so that the people you are caring for don't realize that their needs are overwhelming you. You're being brave because you haven't seen an alternative to being stoic and solid and always available to others.

I wish I knew which past hurt echoes through your soul today. You don't put it out there in conversation, even with close friends, because you think it would surprise and baffle people that the most poignant pain you ruminate over isn't the accident, illness, loss, or other "defining moment" that haunts you most. I'm not surprised. I understand that seemingly small hurts are the easiest ones to carry around in your heart's pocket and revisit every free moment.

I wish I knew what worry makes your heart skip a beat each time you step outside of your comfort zone. How the offhand comments of another leave your mouth dry and your palms sweaty. I imagine you have days that ticktock along like years because your energy is spent pretending you're fine and your hope is spent on survival instead of healing.

I wish you knew how much I pray to the One who does know every bit about you and who holds you in a great, protective embrace. Maybe this would bring you comfort. Maybe this would encourage you to allow that embrace to save you along this journey.

Shedding Light

- Who in your life doesn't know that the love of God is a personal, transforming love?
- Consider the way you hide your own loneliness or pain... most people you meet have those same hurts. Extend grace to those you encounter today.
- You can't always know what someone is going through, but God does. Trust his leading.

Prayer

Lord, I pray for those who have pain so deep that they barely make it through the day. Remove their loneliness and help them to seek out your heart and unconditional love. Give me a heart that is in line with your own so that I can offer up the right words and right actions people need.

Afterglow

When someone lashes out or pulls back, I will not take it personally, but will cover them in prayer.

*Light a Candle
for Possibility*

Birthing Pains

*Each day you must say to yourself,
"Today I am going to begin."*

JEAN PIERRE DE CAUSSADE

This is the year. My friends and I have felt that this could be the year we do more than merely contemplate and mull over our ideas. This could be the time in our lives when we put our ideas out into the world and see what can come of them.

The life of an idea begins at conception, but the power and influence of that idea begins when we send out the birth announcements. Unfortunately, many of us prolong the gestation period. Procrastinators, late bloomers, or those who believe they're not original, creative, or smart are the women with the longest gestations. Sorry to say this, but we're the elephants of the idea world. But I also have some good news for us. We, the plotters and the planners, are often the ones who give birth to the largest, strongest, most fascinating ideas. We just have to be willing to go through the labor pains.

Why is putting forth our ideas so painful, anyway? Why is it that we become afraid for our ideas to see the light of day? Personally, sometimes I'm afraid that the world will take one look at my idea and call it ugly...unworthy...puny. I believe that somewhere along the way we have forgotten that our ideas are part of God's creative purpose for our lives.

Follow through with the birthing of those ideas that grow within. You've been carrying them and protecting them. Now it's time to push them forth. Don't worry about what others will say about them. Just love them. Nurture them. See them as a wonderful, exciting extension of you, your heart, and the One who made you.

Shedding Light

- Are you gestating like an elephant? Isn't it time to birth that idea?

- Ideas aren't intended to be born full grown. They are supposed to be out in the world for a while before they are mobile or speak to others. You'll be able to nurture them as they grow.

- What holds you back from pushing your dreams forward?

Prayer

God, you give me dreams big and small. Guide me to follow your leading as I strive toward them. Connect me with others who will also nurture the dreams you want to see unfold in my life. May I strive to bring forth things of goodness and worth in your eyes.

Afterglow

This is the year...the week...the day, even...that I will give life to a new idea or to one that I've held close to my heart for far too long.

What to Pack for Time Travel

Lives based on having are less free than
lives based on either doing or being.

WILLIAM JAMES

It's midnight and I await 12:01 to mark the start of a new year. Straddling two years makes me feel like a time traveler. I hear fireworks. (I always wonder who sends those lights and sounds skyward for the holiday.) And yet there have been many eves on which I've been in the REM state of slumber when the actual changeover from old to new has taken place. I never thought I missed out on much, but I was wrong. When I stay awake and ponder what it means to begin again, I discover a great sense of optimism. Who are we if not beings who like beginnings? We don't always enjoy the work involved with starting over, but the appeal of a fresh start is strong for most of us.

Make the most of a new day. Apply a rush of optimism to aspects of your life that are staid and stagnant. If you are standing on the dividing line between what is past and what can be, how do you hope things will be different as you step fully into the present and set your sights on the future? What or whom should you let go of? I like to examine those things I should pare away from my attitude (sarcasm, apathy) and my possessions (clothes, unused workout equipment). Then it is fruitful to prayerfully consider what I should be adding to my life in the form of activities (volunteer opportunities), concerns (community health care), and dreams (travel, write).

Life is precious. Don't wait for the transition to a new year to consider what you can get rid of, what you are lacking, and what you are grateful for. Every morning you are traveling through time…it happens to be through your today. Only carry with you that which matters. And don't regret leaving a few things in the care of yesterday.

Shedding Light

- Think of one of your beginnings and how much it added to your life. What did it lead to?

- Do you straddle yesterday and today? Make the jump to today and see what you can do when your priorities and sensibilities are not divided.

- What do you think God wants you to leave behind? What are you supposed to take with you as you move forward?

Prayer

This or that? That or this? God, help me decide what to take with me as I press on toward possibility. Fill me with the light of optimism. I want to cherish my time, I want to savor my life, I want to live the gift of today.

Afterglow

I'll make a fresh start today and embrace the possibility of possibility!

Not a Spirit of Timidity

Don't trust to hold God's hand; let Him hold yours.
Let Him do the holding, and you the trusting.

HAMMER WILLIAM WEBB-PEPLOE

What's with the humidity in this room? Maybe I can leave early, I think as beads of sweat emerge at my hairline and along the curve of my neck. *Why did I come? Isn't it hot in here?* My throat is dry. This isn't an airborne disease entering my system. This is the power of timidity taking over my sense of courage and value at a social function. I don't have breakdowns, mind you. I tend to hold my own at gatherings, but typically a sense of dread rather than anticipation covers me when joining a group of most any kind. The symptoms kick in: awkwardness, fatigue, and a sense of fight or flight that takes over my thought process and apparently my sweat glands.

Can you relate? For many women, timidity can be the shadow that covers their moments to shine and to grow. It pulls them back when they are ready to express their opinions, heart, ideas, or their faith. Timidity can feel like the humidity of the Gulf Coast, but it isn't something we acclimate to or move away from. It follows us wherever we go until we take on God's strength and become empowered to be the unique, valued individual we have been created to be. God doesn't want us to hold back; he wants us to express who we are and who he is with passion and confidence. I have no problem voicing my opinion, yet I give over my confidence to that warped voice inside that says I'm not the person I should be. Send that warped voice out for ice and listen for the still, small voice of God. He'll set you straight and tell you *You are loved. You are mine. You have my strength. It's time to shine.*

Shedding Light

- Which situations stir up your timidity? How have you handled those times in the past?

- What does your warped inner voice say sometimes? What is God saying above (or below) the din of that negative narrator?

- Know without a doubt that you are loved, you are God's child, and you live in his strength.

Prayer

I trust you with my days, God. I can barely see beyond the current hour, but you see through eternity. I give you every part of me. Do something—anything—with this spirit of timidity I've adopted. I'm ready to step into your purpose with divine confidence.

Afterglow

I will not be afraid of the times I am supposed to shine.

Who Needs Whom?

God does not die when we cease to believe in a personal deity, but we die on the day when our lives cease to be illuminated by the steady radiance, renewed daily, of a wonder, the source of which is beyond all reason.

DAG HAMMARKSKJÖLD

As you make choices, care for your family, and plot plans for the future, whose guidance are you seeking daily? When trouble rains down and your heart is laden with sorrow, whom do you trust to see you through to better times? As fear creeps into your rare moments of silence, whom do you turn to for peace? We quickly respond with "God, of course," because we do have faith. We know that God loves us and cares for us. We *know* this. But do we *live* as though we believe it?

Our time on this earth is amazingly precious and uncertain. Let's face it, we step out onto the front porch and we don't know what will happen next in our day. We can guess. We can hope. But we don't know. Doesn't it make sense to seek the leading of our all-knowing Creator? When we are waiting for faith to run deep in our lives, it is not because God needs time to become more real, more omniscient, more powerful. God has been God for a long time. He isn't waiting for us to truly believe in him before he can finally get some work done in the world. When we wait to believe completely, we miss our chance to live in God's purpose. When we leave everything to whimsy, emotion, or our own strength, we miss out on God's leading and clarity.

The current of "unknowing" in our lives is not meant to sweep us to places of fear and failure. The unknowing is the miracle that leads us to the wonder and mystery of a God who cares for us. Don't just know of God and about God; live in God. Experience the excitement and possibility lying beneath life's uncertainties when you wholly trust the known God.

Shedding Light

- When you disconnect from God's leading, he remains the Almighty…but you lose the power of the Creator in your life. Stay in touch with him. Remain linked to his strength and intention.

- Whims are fun to pursue for a Saturday afternoon, but not for a lifetime. Don't let your emotions rule your life. God has so much planned for it.

- Embrace the "unknowing" as a chance to trust God with every decision and every hope.

Prayer

I want my faith to run deep and true. God, show me the possibility of living in your purpose, even as I face uncertainty.

Afterglow

I will live as one who knows wholly and completely and without a doubt that God loves me.

Light at the End
of the Tunnel Vision

When one door closes, another opens, but we often
look so long and so regretfully upon the closed door
that we do not see the one which has opened for us.

ALEXANDER GRAHAM BELL

Have you ever gone back and retouched a resolution, so that you appeared to be closer to your aspiration? That never satisfies (not that I've tried such a thing, of course). It is quite unfortunate when we stand and stare at the path not taken, the job not explored, the relationship never initiated. These "undone" things feel more like losses than missed opportunities. We carry these perceived losses around with us, giving them weight and a sense of reality. But they are not truths, and they certainly shouldn't dictate your future or your today.

God must be saddened when he shines his light on our lives and sees us frozen with fear, big eyed, and unable to move toward the illuminated path. We are startled by a new direction being presented! It takes us by surprise because our eyes have been fixed on the things never pursued. I've never loved the pithy remark "When God closes a door, he opens a window." Why would God open a window when he can take the roof off of our house of cards? I don't think God goes to a downsized dream that fits through a smaller portal. This is the point in life when we should watch for the big hopes of a wide-open faith.

Be ready to move forward. And be prepared to leave a few things behind. Release your hold on regret; it won't serve you or God in the new venture. Decline an attitude of defeat; it doesn't belong in victorious living. Let go of last year's longings; they won't fit the new you. Now follow the light that radiates toward your future.

Shedding Light

- Are you afraid of what lies ahead? Even as God shines a light on your future? Take one step toward the horizon.

- Watch God take the roof off of your situation…in a good way. He'll reveal the expanse of the stars and the wonder of wide-open faith.

- Can you remove those "undone" things from your list of regrets? Allow them to be catalysts to embrace what you will do under God's leading.

Prayer

God, you define me. I won't give power over to the paths not taken…they lead nowhere! I will give power over to your vision and the light you shine on the way up ahead.

Afterglow

Today I will not consider defeat an option. I will be excited about and aware of how God is unfolding my life's potential.

Permission for Possibility

Your life is something opaque, not transparent,
as long as you look at it in an ordinary human way.
But if you hold it up against the light of God's goodness,
it shines and turns transparent, radiant and bright.

ALBERT SCHWEITZER

One day my husband told me that if something ever happened to him, I should quit my job, sell the house, and move to Paris to live and write for a year or more. I said, "Oh, don't talk like that," and then I said, "Thank you." I liked his dream for me because it suits me. And it meant that he was thinking about my passions. Later, I set aside the without-my-husband part of that scenario and took time to ponder what I would do with possibility. Travel. Write. Purge my belongings. Evaluate my priorities. Then I considered what I can do with possibility today—each and every one of those things! Yet why don't I?

How are you at pursuing the things on your heart? What are the leadings that drift in and out of your thoughts and prayers and times of silence, even when brief? Is your list similar to mine or radically different? Maybe you are one of the bold and courageous women who has strived to embrace her potential for many years.

All I know is that we need to stop tying our dreams to the anchor of impossibility and start whisking them along with the

---

wings of possibility. God is the Creator and Fulfiller of endless opportunities, dreams, and visions. We should believe in horizons that open up our lives in ways that surpass our imaginations and hopes. Such experiences are the work of God. His signature is all over brilliant dreams realized. And his hope is behind ordinary dreams brilliantly realized.

I want us to taste that life beyond the excuses. No, I want us to breathe it, embrace it, and ultimately dive headfirst (noses not even plugged) into that life beyond doubt. Not that you need it, but you do hereby have my permission to dream and perceive possibility as a requirement for really living.

Shedding Light

- When you are alone with your thoughts and dreams… what are they?

- Do you give each day the weight it deserves? It is an entire day's worth of dreaming, living, and being as a child of God. It is significant!

- Release your hopes from the anchors of negativity and impossibility.

Prayer

Sometimes my hopes feel limited. It is almost as though I've given up on bigger dreams. I want to be alive with excitement and motivation again, God. I renew my hope in your brilliance. I renew my strength in your divine design.

Afterglow

I will hold my life up to the light of God's goodness.

Light a
Candle for the
Journey

Moving On

It takes some of us a lifetime to learn that Christ,
our Good Shepherd, knows exactly what He is
doing with us. He understands us perfectly.

PHILLIP KELLER

When my third grade teacher announced to my Iowa grade school class that I was moving to Oregon, she pulled down a large United States map, blue and green like the sea. She first pointed to Iowa, nestled comfortably in the middle, and then to a location so far on the left that she had to stretch her arm to reach it. It seemed about as far from my childhood spot in the universe as Mars. It was a visual that reinforced what I already felt emotionally. *I'm leaving the center of the world.* Who wants to say goodbye to the life they have known and start over?

As an adult I have several friends who have had to make big moves. A couple of them faced significant geographic jumps (I resisted unveiling a vinyl map and pointing out just how far they were going), and the other had to make big shifts in career pursuits. They each faced the big task and trial of sifting through belongings. From shredding old bills and filing photos to wrapping vases in bubble wrap, they prepared to pare down life so that they were flexible enough to embark on a journey.

These times of moving on are difficult physically and spiritually. We grow roots in community, in familiarity, and in security. These are all good and vital to our survival. But times of uprooting and transition are also part of survival and of goodness. When you can embrace a change in time zone rather than linger in your comfort zone, you will discover God's provision. When you can press on during a change in direction, you will discover God's faithfulness. When you are able to make God the center of your world instead of yourself, you are making strides toward a plan and purpose...even when you have to stretch your life to reach it.

Shedding Light

- Are you having to stretch your life so far that it hurts spiritually, emotionally, and physically right now? Have you ever?

- Do you trust God as the Shepherd of your life yet?

- Can you view changes in direction, location, or life patterns as a faith adventure? Each kind of change is a chance to grow in faith and discover the depths to which you can depend on God.

Prayer

Lord, I'm giving you my days, my needs, my choices, and my trust. Faith can be a bit scary, but I'm in this for good. I will walk in your way, and I will reach out to embrace the adventure of a lifetime.

Afterglow

I will view change as an opportunity to live more intentionally and to trust God more faithfully.

Escape Routes

*It helps me if I remember that God is
in charge of my day—not I.*

CHARLES R. SWINDOLL

Backup plans are nice, even practical and healthy. I consider myself extremely mature and wise when I think through the best and worst case scenarios of a situation and chart out another path to success. But what is going on when we jump from strategically mapping out a backup plan to cleverly plotting a back *out* plan?

You might be someone who follows through with every commitment and who never thinks in terms of finding the nearest exit when facing obligations or those events and activities that make you uncomfortable. But I bring this up because I personally like to have an escape route when I face a new situation or when I attend a gathering. There are times when I've scheduled another appointment after an event so that I have a forced cutoff point. I often rejoice when an activity is canceled, because when I get out of something I have a surge of excitement. It feels like a snow day in grade school. I anticipate the free time and the possibilities of how I'll fill it.

However, as rebellious and whimsical as they feel initially, our back out plans eventually black out our dates of availability for what God has planned for us. If we dictate exactly how our life should unfold, we are never open to what God's plan is for us. If we spend our energy searching for an "out," we will never be in God's will. When you step in to each new situation with an open mind and open heart, you will get the most out of it.

Let's put our energy toward mapping a way out of mindsets and habits that keep our lives restricted and controlled. It will be the greatest escape of all.

Shedding Light

- Do you ever hope that events will be canceled or that you can bow out of a commitment?

- How have you tried to escape responsibilities or relationships? Why did you have that impulse?

- Entering a new situation is easier when you release control of the outcome. I know that's hard to do, but it works. Try it with something you are facing this week.

Prayer

God, you are the only backup and safety net I need. Help me to resist placing my expectations on people and moments of my life. I want to greet each possibility with an open mind and a trusting heart.

Afterglow

I will spend time praying for and mapping out a way to leave behind fear and move forward in faith.

Just Visiting

*Teach us to number our days and recognize how
few they are; help us to spend them as we should.*

PSALM 90:12 TLB

This past year I had the wonderful opportunity to spend time in my birth state and town and also in the city where I lived after college. One is small-town America and the other is an urban expanse of blocks. During my nostalgic visits, the simplest things triggered a deep sense of joy. A field of corn set against a darkened summer storm sky. A girls' softball game and the aroma of hot dogs from the snack shack. The brick building where I had my first career position. The boarded-up windows of a deli and pie shop that used to be my regular breakfast stop. The pine plank–floored bedroom in my first childhood home. Each piece of my past was enjoyable real estate to walk through, but it also felt good to just be visiting. Not because I couldn't see myself in these places again, but because we should never take up residence in days gone by.

You might not walk along the town square of your youth, but maybe you frequently return to a past incident, a time of suffering or affliction, or even a happy time that you've been trying unsuccessfully to recapture. There is much to learn from the earlier legs of our journeys. Why do we have the humor we do? Why do we say our *R*s or *O*s with a bit of an accent?

It's good to notice the things we have adopted permanently into our personality or our sense of priority, but we are never meant to live in our past.

God lives with you in the present. This morning is the one in which he greets you with leading and love. This afternoon God will plant a seed of hope in your situation of concern. This evening is when he eases your concerns and reminds you in the quiet of your many blessings. Today God is shaping you. Don't be tempted to live anywhere else.

Shedding Light

- Where do you reside during your day or sleepless nights? Are you lost in a past circumstances, or are you living out today as God leads?

- Think on those things that you are grateful to have brought along from your past…good habits, sensibilities, faith, etc.

Prayer

God, usher me into the present when I linger over the past too often or for too long. When I revisit my hurts, remind me of my healing. When I start to wish for times gone by to resurface… remind me that today is where you and I connect and where you are guiding my steps.

Afterglow

I will take up residence in my life as it is now so that I can celebrate what happens today and have hope in tomorrow.

What's Left Is the Living

*If you wish to possess finally all that is
yours, give yourself entirely to God.*

HADEWIJCH OF BRABANT

Imaginary Counselor: How are you doing since we last met?

You: I've been reaching out to others more and more. And I've
been going to God for gratitude.

IC: What are you giving back to God?

You: Like an offering?

IC: When you give to God, you open up your life to God's
abundance. What are you lifting up to God that matters
to you?

You: I might be a bit more grateful, but life is far from perfect.
How can I give to God when I've still got all of this…

IC: What? What holds you back?

You: I've got a lot of anger. I'm not proud of it. What could I
possibly give to God when my heart is hardened?

IC: You answered your question. Give God that anger.

You: That's brokenness and bitterness. That's not a gift.

IC: Oh, but it is. When something consumes you, it steals your heart away from God. When you give that anger to God, the true offering is what remains.

You: That can't be much. If I gave up that heartbreak and rage, I'd be empty. What good is that?

IC: Would you be empty or free?

You: Well, free I guess. But there's the void from the anger…

IC: What remains?

You: Just me.

IC: Exactly. This is the offering God has been waiting for.

Shedding Light

- Give your anger, regret, and other life barriers to God.
- How long have you put off giving all of yourself to God?
- God knows what you are clinging to for false security. Accept the peace of being known and give the rest of your days to God's leading.

Prayer

This is it…my worst and my best. I give you my excuses, fear, and any anger that has kept me from love and gratitude. I give you this day along with my future hope.

Afterglow

Even when I don't feel like I have much to give, I'll give everything I am to God.

Rebirth

*When I look at the galaxies on a clear night—when
I look at the incredible brilliance of creation, and
think that this is what God is like, then instead
of feeling intimidated and diminished by it, I
am enlarged...I rejoice that I am a part of it.*

MADELEINE L'ENGLE

Nobody wants to hear about or think about death. Our culture often deals with death through the method of denial. And the more we leave a topic to grow in a corner like the shadow monsters of our childhood, the less we're able to cope with it in a healthy way. Are you waiting for something uplifting? I have it to offer, I really do. A friend and I were talking about the idea of death being the beginning of new life...a rebirth. This friend had lost someone quickly. There wasn't time to ponder and reflect; she had to just "be" with this person whom she loved and help him die. It was a time of sadness but not of fear because she honored her friend's life and death by providing tenderness, stories, laughter, and her presence during his last days. She helped him let go of the world and embrace new life.

We shouldn't let anything take away the beauty of this rebirth. Not fear, not ignorance, not shame. The denial of our inevitable physical demise prevents us from seeing death as a significant, meaningful part of life. When you look to the sky and contemplate God and the universe…you are a part of it all. The wonder. The miracle. Do you realize that death is our last offering to God? It's the point in our journey when we can say, "Take me into your presence, Lord." And this "me" is the part of us that loves others, delights in a sunset, praises God for life, and prays to God for guidance—this is the "me" who knows the hurt of brokenness and the joy of healing and who is ready to be whole and wholly in the presence of God. A new being, a new beginning.

Shedding Light

- Nurture your soul and your connection to God.
- Honor the importance of a second birth.
- Don't give death the power that life is meant to have. When you deny the fact of death, you give it the force of fear.

Prayer

God, even now I can give you all of myself daily by trusting you and staying in communion with you. I know that you mourn our deaths, our suffering, and our limited time on earth…but you also welcome us into your presence forever. Thank you for the comfort of knowing that our last offering is lovingly received.

Afterglow

I will savor living in God's presence today so that I might understand the peace that will cover me when I face a second birth.

Potluck Faith in Action

*Delight yourself in the Lord and he will
give you the desires of your heart.*

PSALM 37:4

That vision I had about hosting a potluck…well, it materialized. And, of course, it had nothing to do with me and
my planning. It was all God's doing. I'm sure he realized that
if I was ever going to put that idea in motion, it would take
many months and maybe even some counseling. As much as
I wanted to open up my home and life to others, I also knew
I'd have to give up control and the need for things to be perfect. What took place was so much better because it was out
of my control. All I had to do was say yes to the opportunity
God carved out for me.

And wouldn't ya know it, this all came about on Christmas Day.

Snow and ice made the driving conditions unsafe for my
husband and me to travel to be with family, so on Christmas
Eve we made our final decision to remain at home. Then we
called a few friends who were also staying in town and invited
them to Christmas dinner.

I was full of gratitude for our home, friends, and for God's
profound presence in our lives during the past year. All day I
was aware that on a small, manageable scale the potluck vision

had materialized. It wasn't the big chaotic event I first envisioned (and been scared by). It was a time of fellowship that unfolded simply and graciously. I know it is just the beginning of how that dream will take shape in my life.

Over time, God forms the desires of our hearts and also orchestrates how they will appear. It might take us a moment to recognize a longing fulfilled, a hope met, a prayer answered, but these realized dreams are appearing all the time. In the light of God's goodness and hope, you will see them for what they are: a gathering of gifts for your faith journey.

Shedding Light

- How has God unfolded a hope that has been on your heart? Take time to reflect on these happenings. They are not by accident. They are purposed, significant gifts.

- Do you have desires of the heart? Sometimes we operate on autopilot for so long that we forget to dream and to nurture those hopes. Give yourself time to consider what God is placing on your heart.

Prayer

Give me a heart for the desires and plans you have for me, God. May I greet each day as another 24 hours in which I can delight in those desires.

Afterglow

I will hold on to the hopes and dreams God gives to me…and I will move forward toward them with gratitude.

About the Author

Hope Lyda has worked in publishing for 12 years and is the author of several novels, including *Life, Libby, and the Pursuit of Happiness,* in addition to numerous nonfiction titles, such as the popular One-Minute Prayers series (more than 600,000 copies sold) and *Tea Light Moments for a Woman's Soul.* When Hope isn't helping others in their writing endeavors as an editor, she can be found working on her latest writing project at a local coffee shop or jotting down ideas on 3 x 5 cards or any piece of scrap paper that's handy. She and her husband live in Oregon, where they enjoy the relaxed lifestyle and beauty of the Northwest and the opportunity to head to the coast at a moment's notice.

You can email Hope at
hopelyda@yahoo.com

or visit her at
www.hopelyda.com

Other inspirational books
by Hope Lyda

One Minute with God
One Minute with God for Women
Prayers of Comfort for Those Who Hurt
Tea Light Moments for a Woman's Soul
One-Minute Prayers™
One-Minute Prayers™ for Healing
One-Minute Prayers™ for Women
One-Minute Prayers™ for Wives
One-Minute Prayers™ to Start Your Day
One-Minute Prayers™ to End Your Day